The Black Ar

THE GREATEST SHOW IN THE GALAXY

By Dale Smith

Published August 2023 by Obverse Books

Cover Design © Cody Schell

Icon Design © Blair Bidmead

Text © Dale Smith, 2023

Editors: Stuart Douglas, Philip Purser-Hallard

Lyrics from 'Bedroom Demo' courtesy of Blade & 691 Influential

Dale Smith has asserted his right to be identified as the author of this Work in accordance with the Copyright, Designs and Patents Act 1988.

All rights reserved. No part of this publication may be reproduced, stored in a retrieval system, or in any form or by any means, without the prior permission in writing of the publisher, nor be otherwise circulated in any form of binding, cover or e-book other than which it is published and without a similar condition including this condition being imposed on the subsequent publisher.

Recently Published

CONTENTS

OVERVIEW

Serial Title: *The Greatest Show in the Galaxy*

Writer: Alan Wareing

Director: Stephen Wyatt

Original UK Transmission Dates: 14 December 1988 – 4 January 1989

Running Time: Part One: 24m 23s

Part Two: 24m 20s

Part Three: 24m 30s

Part Four: 24m 24s

UK Viewing Figures: Part One: 5.0 million

Part Two: 5.3 million

Part Three: 4.9 million

Part Four: 6.6 million

Regular Cast: Sylvester McCoy (The Doctor), Sophie Aldred (Ace)

Guest Cast: TP McKenna (Captain Cook), Jessica Martin (Mags), Ricco Ross (Ringmaster), Ian Reddington (Chief Clown), Peggy Mount (Stallslady), Gian Sammarco (Whizzkid), Daniel Peacock (Nord), Christopher Guard (Bellboy), Deborah Manship (Morgana), Chris Jury (Deadbeat), Dee Sadler (Flower Child), Dean Hollingsworth (Bus Conductor), David Ashford (Dad), Janet Hargreaves (Mum), Kathryn Ludlow (Little Girl)

Antagonists: The Chief Clown, the Gods of Ragnarok

Novelisation: *Doctor Who: The Greatest Show in the Galaxy* by Stephen Wyatt. **The Target Doctor Who Library** #144.

Critical Responses:

'This is everything **Doctor Who** should be.'

[Tat Wood, *About Time 6*]

'If one wishes to be picky, there is practically no script. It is just an awful lot of meetings with the assorted characters.'

[David J Richardson, Fanzine review[1]]

---

[1] Unknown fanzine, co-edited by Bill Edmunds of New Hampshire, according to Richardson's website.

SYNOPSIS

Part One

In a circus ring, **the Ringmaster** raps 'You ain't seen nothing yet!'.

The **Chief Clown**, dressed as an undertaker, tracks the runaways **Flowerchild** and **Bellboy** in a hearse with dark-tinted windows. Flowerchild shelters in an abandoned bus where she finds a strange box, only to be killed by the bus' robot **Conductor**. Unnoticed, one of her earrings falls to the ground as the Conductor drags her body away. The Chief Clown uses kites to find Bellboy and returns him to the circus.

The Doctor and **Ace** take up an invitation from a junk mail droid and visit the Psychic Circus on Segonax, in spite of the fact Ace is frightened of clowns. The planet is desolate and seemingly empty, except for the ill-tempered **owner of a roadside stall**, and **Nord**, a foul-mouthed biker. Later, walking towards the Circus, they encounter **Captain Cook** and **Mags**, two intergalactic explorers. At their campsite, a partially buried **robot** attacks them, but Ace disables it with a shovel.

Elsewhere, **Whizzkid**, a young boy with spectacles, arrives on his bicycle and sets off for the Circus.

The four travellers come across the abandoned bus, where the Conductor attacks them. The Doctor incapacitates it and Ace finds Flowerchild's lost earring and pins it to her jacket. Unimpressed by Captain Cook, the Doctor and Ace press on towards the Circus alone.

Mags and Captain Cook watch Bellboy dragged into the ring for punishment. Mags screams but the Ringmaster uses a device to deaden the sound. Even so, Ace hears the scream, though the Doctor does not. He asks Ace to decide whether they should enter the Circus.

Part Two

Inside the Circus, the Doctor and Ace discover that the entire audience comprises a single family, of a **father**, **mother** and young **daughter**.

They speak to **Morgana**, a fortune teller and one of original members of the Circus, before the Doctor takes up an invitation to perform. Taken backstage, he joins Captain Cook, Mags and Nord in a caged waiting area. Cook explains their lives are at stake in the talent competition – failure to please the audience will lead to their death. After Cook tricks Nord into performing next, his attempt to tell a joke falls flat and he is killed.

Meanwhile, the Chief Clown has recognised Flowerchild's earring on Ace's jacket and asks where she got it. Ace runs away from him, deeper into the Circus.

Whizzkid arrives and is revealed to be a huge fan of the Circus and of Captain Cook. He too wishes to enter the talent show. When he is escorted backstage, they discover that the Doctor and Mags, have escaped. **Deadbeat**, an odd job man, watches on.

The Doctor and Mags follow a series of stone corridors to a deep pit, at the bottom of which is an enormous alien eye. Before they can investigate further, Captain Cook arrives with some of the clowns to take them back to the circus ring to perform.

Part Three

After overcoming the damaged robots, Ace discovers that Bellboy is also in the repair room. He recognises Flowerchild's ear-ring and explains that he created all the robots in the Circus and she the kites, but that their ideals had been twisted and abused once the Circus fell under the control of an unseen force. He gives Ace a remote control for his masterpiece, the large semi-buried android they encountered earlier.

The Doctor has escaped his guard and arrives with Deadbeat. Bellboy reminds Deadbeat that his real name is **Kingpin**, and that he is the Circus' original leader. While Bellboy attempts to delay the pursuing clowns, the Doctor, Ace and the newly renamed Kingpin make their way back to the pit and the glaring eye. Kingpin collapses after showing them that the eye is connected to a mirrored eye amulet he wears. The amulet is incomplete, however. – the eye at its centre lacks an eyeball. They realise the missing eyeball must have been in the abandoned bus and that Flowerchild died trying to retrieve it. The Doctor sends Ace and Kingpin to find the eyeball while he tries to buy them time by taking his turn in the ring, following on from the unsuccessful Whizzkid.

The Doctor suggests to Mags and Captain Cook that they work together in the ring and they agree, but as soon as they begin their show, Cook causes Mags to transform into a snarling werewolf who attacks the Doctor.

Part Four

While the Doctor attempts to elude the transformed Mags, Ace and Deadbeat return to the bus, destroy the conductor and find the missing eyeball. Mags savages Captain Cook and she and the Doctor escape. With no more acts available, the audience turns on the Ringmaster and Morgana, and they are killed by the clowns.

As Ace and Deadbeat make their way back with the now complete amulet, the Doctor steps into another dimension and confronts the power which controls the Circus, the three **Gods of Ragnarök**. He does magic tricks to amuse them while Ace uses the remote control given to her by Bellboy to destroy the clowns and then throws the amulet down the pit where the Doctor catches it.

Using its power, the Doctor destroys both the Gods and the Circus tent, which explodes behind him as he calmly walks away.

WHAT DID YOU SAY YOUR NAME WAS?

The title for *The Greatest Show in the Galaxy* [2] (1988-89) was suggested by Producer John Nathan-Turner at his initial script meeting with writer Stephen Wyatt and Script Editor Andrew Cartmel in May 1988 [3]. A play on the Barnum and Bailey Circus' enduring billing as 'The Greatest Show on Earth', it was a title that Cartmel was not particularly sold on[4], but nonetheless it is possible to see why it appealed to Nathan-Turner: the *Radio Times* printed 'Doctor Who: The Greatest Show In the Galaxy' in its listings for four weeks[5]. But in some ways the title can be seen as more than just an expression of Nathan-Turner's eye for publicity: despite Cartmel's dislike of it, it can be read as his statement of intent for the show.

Although *The Greatest Show* was broadcast last in Season 25, this was caused by coverage of the Seoul Olympics and Nathan-Turner's insistence that *Silver Nemesis* (1988) – ostensibly the 25th Anniversary story – should be broadcast as close to 23 November as possible[6]. It was the second story of the season to be produced, after

---

[2] Hereafter, for reasons of space, *The Greatest Show*.

[3] *Doctor Who: The Complete History* (TCH) #45, p56. 'John's title; we let him have it; it made him happy.' (Cartmel, Andrew, *Script Doctor: The Inside Story of Doctor Who 1986-89*, p134).

[4] 'A title I never liked and one that is ironically unworthy of the show it denotes' (Cartmel, *Script Doctor*, p132). Given that Cartmel is generally complimentary about the story and his version of **Doctor Who** in the book, I can only assume the 'show' he is referring to here is the Psychic Circus.

[5] 'Programme Index'. *BBC Genome*, 14 December 1988.

[6] TCH #45, p83. The first of *Silver Nemesis*'s three episodes was broadcast on Wednesday 23 November.

the opener *Remembrance of the Daleks* (1988), and as such marks the point at which Cartmel's reinvigoration of the show can be called a pattern rather than a fluke.

> '*The Greatest Show in the Galaxy* represented a watershed in my thinking on **Doctor Who** [...] I felt we were providing first rate scripts and providing them for the best incarnation of the Doctor in years, if not decades.'[7]

However, the story wasn't seen by large numbers of the viewing public: episode one was the 86th most watched programme of its week, whilst episode three slipped to 108th, before the final episode managed claw its way back to 79th[8]. In an apparent attempt to finish off the show, McCoy's era was scheduled against **Coronation Street** (1960-)[9] – although *The Greatest Show* was the story that received McCoy's highest ratings[10]. Within fandom, it is mostly remembered for a handful of key touchstones and disregarded in favour of more resounding successes like *Remembrance* or the majority of Season 26. It is the one with the creepy clowns, the one that nearly became another *Shada*[11] (1979, unbroadcast), and – because of the inclusion

---

[7] Cartmel, *Script Doctor*, p132.

[8] Sullivan, Shannon Patrick. The Greatest Show in the Galaxy.

[9] 'Moving it against **Coronation Street** was just a way of throwing it away, really,' according to Jonathan Powell. (Quoted in Marson, Richard, *Totally Tasteless: the Life of John Nathan-Turner*, p247).

[10] Wood, Tat, *About Time: The Unauthorized Guide to Doctor Who Volume 6 – Seasons 22 to 26, the TV Movie*, pp717-18.

[11] The discovery of asbestos at BBC Television Centre led to the closure of the studio set aside for **Doctor Who**. For a couple of hours the story was officially cancelled, until agreement was reached to set up a tent in a car park at BBC Elstree, thus avoiding a repeat of the

of Gian Simmarco's 'the Whizzkid', a fanatical devotee of the titular Psychic Circus – the one that is most often summed up with the truism 'a show in ratings free-fall probably shouldn't ridicule its core audience.'[12]

The Whizzkid was suggested in response to the second draft of the storyline, and appeared in his original form in the third[13]:

> 'The Whizzkid was a much more important character in earlier drafts. He was going to be the original computer game nerd, but I turned him into a parody of **Doctor Who** fans. It was a bit of a last-minute, on-the-spot improvisation.'[14]

The Complete History suggests that John Nathan-Turner particularly enjoyed this development, stating he liked the 'barker' – which was a term he used to refer to obsessive fans of **Doctor Who**, presumably through a connection with the phrase 'barking mad'[15]. But just what was it he found so appealing about this representation of the kind of fan he and Eric Saward had spent so long pitching **Doctor Who** at?

---

cancellation mid-filming which befell *Shada* in 1979. (TCH #45, pp71-72).

[12] Wood, *About Time 6,* p715.

[13] Griffiths, Peter, 'Honk, the Squonk and a Green Non-Entity', *Doctor Who Magazine* (DWM) #263.

[14] Stephen Wyatt in Griffiths, Peter, 'Oh What a Circus Oh What a Show', DWM #263.

[15] TCH #45, p60; Cartmel, *Script Doctor,* p26. In this case, the expression is a little open to confusion, since 'barker' is a well-known term for a carnival showman and would therefore apply instead to the Ringmaster.

There is a rumour in fan circles that the Whizzkid was based on future showrunner Chris Chibnall[16], after he upset Pip and Jane Baker during an edition of **Open Air** (1986) by describing 'The Ultimate Foe' (1986) as 'silly' and 'routine'[17] – a rumour I have sadly to quash[18]. Whilst this may not be true, the stereotype that the Whizzkid plays on – one 'obsessively devoted to a certain pursuit' – was well established by the 1950s and hasn't changed much since[19]. Certainly – as Nathan-Turner's dismissive nickname suggests – the **Doctor Who** production office had come into contact with its fair share of fans who could probably assume the Whizzkid was a personal dig at them. The cruelty of the jibe seemed particularly pronounced as Nathan-Turner had always courted fan approval: when he took over as Producer, he began a campaign of bringing the fans onboard, going so far as to brief against his immediate predecessor Graham Williams and push the idea that the Nathan-Turner era was a return to the golden age of the show after a descent into pantomime and silliness[20]. Only three years before, he had been encouraging the

---

[16] Raised, for example, in Ranger, 'We May Laugh Yet'.

[17] **Open Air**, episode #1.29. His complaint that the show wasn't significantly different from before the hiatus is fair, but the behind-the-scenes reasons why 'The Ultimate Foe' might not have been the best season finale are explored in detail in James Cooray Smith's excellent *The Black Archive #14: The Ultimate Foe*.

[18] 'I've never heard that. Given that I'd never heard of Chris Chibnall until he became showrunner, I can definitely state he was not in my mind back in 1987.' Stephen Wyatt, author's own interview, 2023.

[19] Tocci, Jason, 'Geek Cultures: Media and Identity in the Digital Age', p18.

[20] Sandifer, Elizabeth, *TARDIS Eruditorum Volume 6: Peter Davison and Colin Baker*, pp22-23; Marson, *Totally Tasteless: The Life of John Nathan-Turner*, p110.

weaponisation of fan outrage after the show was taken off-air for a 'rethink' through his catspaw, Ian Levine[21].

Oh yes, Ian Levine.

Levine is a wealthy **Doctor Who** fan, who in 1985 managed to become the show's unpaid and uncredited continuity advisor. Unbiased accounts of the extent of his duties are hard to come by – both he and Eric Saward argue over which of them actually wrote *Attack of the Cybermen* (1986)[22] – but he certainly contributed to the prevailing shift in the kind of stories that **Doctor Who** told after its 20th anniversary: gradually, it stopped trying to appeal to a wider audience and started mining its own past for inspiration, making stories with one eye on how they would go down at the fan conventions [23]. Learning of the US convention circuit after the cancellation of *Shada*[24], Nathan-Turner thought that inspiring the kind of love and loyalty that **Star Trek** (1966-69) commanded would keep the show popular, unfortunately forgetting that **Star Trek**'s unpopularity with the general public saw it cancelled after only three seasons. **Doctor Who** had survived for 20 by being mass entertainment, but now it yearned to be cult television[25].

---

[21] Sandifer, *TARDIS Eruditorum Volume 6*, p521; Marson, *Totally Tasteless*, pp187-189.

[22] Neither seems to realise that their standing within fandom would be improved by people thinking they'd had nothing to do with it.

[23] Marson, *Totally Tasteless*, pp107-08.

[24] Molesworth, Richard, *The John Nathan-Turner Production Diary 1979-1990*, p23.

[25] Sandifer, *TARDIS Eruditorum Volume 6*, pp509-27.

After the 1985 hiatus, Levine's status changed: instead of standing inside the tent and aiming out, he was unceremoniously thrust outside. He claims to have initiated the parting of the ways in protest at the casting of Bonnie Langford[26]; John Nathan-Turner seemed to lose faith in him after Levine announced news of Season 23's reduced episode count to a convention audience [27]. Levine turned aggressively on Nathan-Turner, and whether he was bringing his people with him or just happened to notice the tide turning, by the time Cartmel was hired John Nathan-Turner's happy relationship with fandom was over[28]. After the show ended, the relationship deteriorated so far that there was a fan-led campaign to remove Nathan-Turner from his job at BBC Enterprises[29]. Is it any wonder that he liked seeing the 'barker' get his comeuppance?

Perhaps that was why Wyatt had the inspiration to make the Whizzkid a **Doctor Who** fan, and why Cartmel kept the change through the further drafts the story went through – another crumb they let John have because it made him happy. But I think there was more to it than that: this was Cartmel's 'watershed' moment, after all. He was, and remains, dismissive of the era of **Doctor Who** immediately preceding his, and – rightly – saw the need for the kind

---

[26] Sandifer, *TARDIS Eruditorum Volume 6*, p506.

[27] Marson, *Totally Tasteless*, pp95-196.

[28] Sandifer, *TARDIS Eruditorum Volume 6*, pp513-514. Molesworth, *John Nathan-Turner Production Diary*, p9.

[29] Molesworth, *John Nathan-Turner Production Diary*, p12. Nathan-Turner maintained it was an argument over a 30th Anniversary BBC Video production that had cost him his job, although his boss at the time remembers that there just wasn't any more for him to do (Marson, *Totally Tasteless*, p270).

of massive change of approach that should have happened immediately after the hiatus. **Doctor Who** had successfully turned itself during the Saward era into cult television made by, and only for, the fans; Cartmel needed to do something to show that his era was different, that **Doctor Who** wasn't just for the fans anymore. What better way could there be than getting one of UK TV's most recognisable child stars[30], having them become just the kind of fan the casual viewer assumed **Doctor Who** was for, and then ritually sacrificing them at 7:35pm on a Wednesday night?

The Whizzkid is killed by the Gods of Ragnarok, but he is put in the ring to face them because Captain Cook shamelessly throws him under the bus, offering his place in the ring to the young fan. And because the Whizzkid is also a fan of Cook – 'I've got maps at home showing all your journeys and a piece of one of your old shoes I bought in a souvenir shop'[31] – he doesn't suspect that he is being used. Of course, his fandom is a clue as to Cook's status in the story – Whizzkid is supposed to be a fan of **Doctor Who**, and so if he is also a fan of Captain Cook, then either his fandom is not a monomania or Cook is in some way connected to **Doctor Who**. Give the old adventurer who goes only by his prefix, with a series of past adventures to recount – specifically ones that are only entertaining to his fan – and a young, female companion who seems to be with him because she is obliged to be rather than out of any great desire, the parallel becomes obvious. As Cartmel says:

---

[30] Sammarco was at the time best known as the titular star of *The Secret Diary of Adrian Mole, Aged 13¾* (1985) and its sequels (TCH #45, p63).

[31] *The Greatest Show in the Galaxy*, Part Three.

'Stephen created Captain Cook as a kind of villainous counterpart to the Doctor – a mysterious space traveller who wanders the galaxies with a female sidekick.'[32]

These kinds of pairings crop up frequently in the Cartmel era – Kane and Belazs in *Dragonfire* (1987), Josiah and Nimrod in *Ghost Light* (1989), the Master and Midge in *Survival* (1989). The punk werewolf Mags was an early suggestion from Andrew Cartmel, who was developing a habit of inserting combative young women into the show whenever he could[33]. But the Captain didn't come into the story until a draft of the first episode had already been written, in a fifth draft storyline that expanded the story to four parts[34]:

'On this occasion we were a bit stuck, and Ben [Aaronovitch] said "Why don't you have an Indiana Jones-type explorer?" That was our starting point. It was only when I started writing the character that I realised he should be a thundering bore, with his cup of tea and his servant.'[35]

The character was intended to be killed off at the end of episode 1, but Wyatt fell in love with him and so he stuck around until the very end[36], even appearing after his death. And it is possible to read his resurrection as another hint: if he is the Doctor, he is a Doctor with an antagonistic relationship with his companion, and a tendency towards boorishness and self-aggrandisement; make it clear that he is dead and gone, only to force him back into playing the same old

---

[32] Cartmel, *Script Doctor*, p139.
[33] Cartmel, *Script Doctor*, p137.
[34] Griffiths, 'Honk, the Squonk and a Green Non-Entity'.
[35] Wyatt in Griffiths, 'Oh What a Circus'.
[36] TCH #45, p59.

role in the same old way because there is no-one else to do it, and it becomes a little on the nose. And he is finally dispatched by the seventh Doctor, which at least parallels the mythology Paul Cornell would eventually work into the **New Adventures**[37], the sequel book series from Virgin Publishing, if not the real story of Colin Baker unwillingly vacating the role[38].

Mags, however, is a little different. She isn't an obvious parallel to any of the companions that came before her, and instead seems more like the companion she shares screen time with: Ace. She is young, spirited and a little bit dangerous, and she has a dark secret that only the Doctor is able to help her come to terms with. And of course Ace befriends her, in that way that Ace frequently befriends young attractive women throughout her time with the Doctor and which Rona Munro picks up on as fuel for the lesbian subtext in *Survival* (1989). It is predominantly her friendship with Ace that allows her to see the true nature of her relationship with the Captain, which is at its heart a colder, more exploitative version of Ace's and the Doctor's, without any of the shared love of anarchy and justice. Or **slightly** more exploitative: whilst Mags gains insight about herself from Ace, the exchange isn't reciprocal. By the end of the story, Mags has earned freedom from the uneven, abusive relationship she found herself trapped in. Ace, however, walks away praising the Doctor for his skilful manipulation.

---

[37] Cornell, Paul, *Love and War*, p48. Although Cornell first put the idea into print in the story 'The Ashes of Our Fathers' in DWAS, *Cosmic Masque* XIV, p28.
[38] Marson, *Totally Tasteless*, pp183-97.

It does seem that *The Greatest Show* is overflowing with parallels to **Doctor Who** itself, to the point where it's hard to imagine they could be accidental. Even the stallholder played by Dame Peggy Mount can be read as connected to the show: she dislikes the Circus but is financially dependent on it, and the fans meekly hand over their money for her products even when they know they won't like them. She sees the trouble the Circus is in – watching Bellboy being dragged away from the clowns – but does nothing to help. The implication here is that she is the story's version of BBC Enterprises, her mixture of sweetcorn and custard whatever latest piece of licensed tat they were expecting fandom to buy[39].

And, of course, the Gods themselves, demanding constant entertainment and offering nothing but scorn and disappointment. They manifest as an idealised 1950s family, something that has been suggested links to the story's theme of the betrayal of the ideals of the 60s[40]: this safe, traditionalist, repressive nuclear family are just what the hippies were rebelling against, and yet the Circus here appeals to them, panders to their whims, in much the same way that the Baby Boomer generation voted in Margaret Thatcher's government, with its aims of stamping out the left and homosexuality in the name of a return to traditional family values. This world was also the one that the Viewers' and Listeners' Association[41] wanted to get back to, an organisation that demanded

---

[39] Stevens, Alan, and Fiona Moore, '47 Cool Things About *The Greatest Show in the Galaxy*', *Celestial Toyroom* #450, 21 October 2015.

[40] Adam and Erik, '*The Greatest Show in the Galaxy*'.

[41] A pressure organisation set up by Mary Whitehouse in 1964 (as the Clean Up TV campaign) that aimed to ensure morality in television

strict boundaries to what was entertaining, and could destroy those who transgressed[42].

However, it is worth pointing out that whilst the Gods of Ragnarok are frequently taken to be a representation of the cruelly indifferent audience watching **Doctor Who**, this doesn't actually marry with the reality of the show. For the entirety of the McCoy era, the casual family audience that the Gods seem to represent weren't watching **Doctor Who** at all: again, the Whizzkid is the more likely representation of the people who were declining the delights of **Coronation Street** in favour of watching the Doctor do his thing. So, in this complex metafiction, just who is this cosy 1950s family supposed to represent?

It has also been suggested that they represent BBC management[43]. Certainly this makes sense of the Doctor's claim that he has 'fought the Gods of Ragnarok all through time'[44] when, as far as the dedicated viewer is concerned, he has never so much as mentioned them before: the only adversaries the Doctor has faced in all incarnations are the Daleks and the BBC itself. It is the Gods of Ragnarok who have taken the Circus and forced it into its reduced circumstances, making increasingly impossible demands for it to entertain, without providing the appropriate means for it to do so. If the Circus does unexpectedly manage to create entertainment –

---

programming, and is widely credited with ending Philip Hinchcliffe's period as Producer on **Doctor Who**. See National Viewers' and Listeners' Association Archive, University of Essex.

[42] Adam and Erik, *'The Greatest Show in the Galaxy'*.

[43] Adam and Erik, *'The Greatest Show in the Galaxy'*; TV Tropes, 'Recap / **Doctor Who** S25 E4 *The Greatest Show in the Galaxy'*.

[44] Part Four.

Nord's near perfect scores as a strongman – the Gods shift the goalposts again to ensure failure – Nord's inability to tell a joke to literally save his life. Indeed, the fact that their reaction to Nord's success is to demand that the show needs more comedy probably isn't a coincidence.

What really signifies the Gods of Ragnarok as BBC management, though, is their reaction to the Whizzkid. They do not share his love for the Circus; they don't even understand it, and they certainly aren't willing to encourage or support it. Instead, their response is to kill the Whizzkid, to destroy the fandom. And they discover to their annoyance that the Doctor himself is not so easy to kill, that even armed only with old-fashioned tricks and stories of good versus evil, he is still powerful enough to endure. At the end of the day, despite everything the Gods throw at him, the Doctor is the one that survives.

But for all that *The Greatest Show* is overflowing with analogues to 1980s **Doctor Who**, that does leave a problem right at its heart. If the Whizzkid is a **Doctor Who** fan – and nobody has ever suggested otherwise – that means that the Psychic Circus itself must also be a representation of the show. Certainly, that seems to be the intention behind the Whizzkid's line 'I never got to see the early days, I know it's not as good as it used to be,'[45] and presenting the Circus as a faded remnant that has lost its connection with its past success, one that inspired so many. Even the transience of the live entertainment the Circus provided is used as a metaphor for the classic stories lost to the BBC's policy of destroying film stock after broadcast, as the Whizzkid waxes lyrical about:

---

[45] Part Three.

'Your tour of the Boreatic Wastes. I think that most of your admirers would agree with me that that was one of your finest ever gigs. Well, in so far as you can tell from the posters.'[46]

But Wyatt introduced another metaphor into the mix with the Circus, one that might be seen as diluting the idea that this is a story about **Doctor Who** itself:

'My starting point was closer to my own experience. In the 1970s I'd been involved in a number of community and children based theatre projects which still drew on an idealistic hippy philosophy of peace and love. Gradually during the 1980s many of the people involved in those projects became more and more involved in mainstream commercial television / theatre. [...] I saw *Greatest Show* as being about the collapse of the hippy dream in response to the commercial and political developments of the late 70s / 80s.'[47]

This idea of the story being about the hippies of the 60s selling out to become the Tories of the 80s resonates with the production team's general anti-Thatcher leanings[48]. However, that is something of a misnomer: the Conservative message of individual freedom without government interference is actually quite a good fit with the hippy ideal of personal enlightenment – although admittedly the rampant consumerism of Thatcherism is less easy to reconcile – and

---

[46] *The Greatest Show in the Galaxy*, Part Two.

[47] Stephen Wyatt, author's own interview.

[48] Wyatt in Griffiths, 'Honk, the Squonk and a Green Non-Entity'; Cartmel, *Script Doctor*, p14.

in any case, while the 'hippie generation' did switch allegiance from Labour to Conservative in 1979, voters in the 18 to 24 age range – the children of the teenagers who would have been hippies in 1967 – also voted more with Thatcher than the previous generation had: the biggest swing from Labour to Conservative in the 1979 election was in the middle classes, regardless of age[49]. Even so, this would seem to confuse the metaphor that the Circus represents **Doctor Who** as a whole... except that **Doctor Who** did have its own representative of the Hippy Generation, one whose association with the show began in 1969 just as the movement was falling apart: John Nathan-Turner[50].

Nathan-Turner was famous for his loud Hawaiian shirts, well-liked and gregarious, popular wherever he went[51]. He faced BBC snobbery and antipathy to **Doctor Who**, and through hard work, talent and an eye for publicity, became the main reason the show didn't disappear when Tom Baker annoyed one too many people[52]. He practised a version of free love, having an open relationship with his partner Gary Downie that saw them sleep with other people, share partners and engage in threesomes[53].

But many of his friends disliked Downie, and saw him as the unpleasant price of being friends with Nathan-Turner: a price that some were unwilling to pay[54]. Nathan-Turner got Downie employed

---

[49] Ipsos, 'How Britain Voted Since October 1974'.
[50] Marson, *Totally Tasteless*, p39.
[51] Cartmel, *Script Doctor*, p90; Marson, *Totally Tasteless*, pp38-42.
[52] Marson, *Totally Tasteless*, pp142-43.
[53] Marson, *Totally Tasteless*, p45.
[54] Marson, *Totally Tasteless*, pp46-48.

at the BBC, to the detriment of his own career; it soon became clear that the two frequently came as a package, and that Downie was not very good at his job[55]. Nathan-Turner tried to get Downie hired as **Doctor Who**'s Production Associate in 1983, and managed to sneak him in as production manager for a handful of stories starting with *The Two Doctors* (1985) – some suspected as a justification for his inclusion and payment as a guest at US conventions[56]. After the production manager had to leave *The Greatest Show*, it was Downie that Nathan-Turner drafted in as a last-minute replacement, to the director's disappointment[57].

At the same time, Nathan-Turner's career stalled. His ambition was to become Controller of BBC One, and almost right from the start he was pitching ideas for his next production after **Doctor Who**. The only one ever to be commissioned was **K9 and Company** (1981), which his superior never seriously considered for a series, despite *A Girl's Best Friend* ostensibly being a pilot for one[58]. Not everyone thought Nathan-Turner was a good producer – Terrance Dicks thought he couldn't 'run a whelk stall'[59] and Christopher Bidmead said he 'didn't even know how television worked'[60] – and not everyone found him easy to get on with. He destroyed his relationship with Nicola Bryant by never apologising for spitting at her after he assumed she had slept with a young gay man he had

---

[55] Marson, *Totally Tasteless*, pp52-54.
[56] Marson, *Totally Tasteless*, pp122, 180, 230.
[57] Marson, *Totally Tasteless*, p253.
[58] Marson, *Totally Tasteless*, pp124-29.
[59] Marson, *Totally Tasteless*, p80.
[60] Marson, *Totally Tasteless*, p82.

befriended[61]. He would demean and belittle the president of the Doctor Who Appreciation Society at public appearances, because he also worked at the BBC and Nathan-Turner suspected him of hunting out and leaking information about upcoming stories: in truth, the source of most of the leaks was Nathan-Turner himself, who would get drunk and loose-lipped with Ian Levine[62].

Nathan-Turner had been unwilling to have anybody working on the show who knew more about it than him, possibly stung by the BBC putting Barry Letts over him as Executive Producer in his first year but more likely because he wanted to put his own stamp on his first series as Producer[63]. Hence Levine finding favour as the – entirely unofficial, unacknowledged and ultimately powerless – repository of **Doctor Who** history. But Nathan-Turner still needed to establish his dominance before Levine would be granted audience:

> 'I remember going to [Nathan-Turner's house at] Brockley early in 1980, and that's the one time I had to get fucked by him – he wouldn't take no for an answer. I had no choice. It was, "You want a favour, I want a favour back."'[64]

In August 1984, Downie and Nathan-Turner invited DWB editor and fan Gary Leigh to their house for dinner. Leigh was warned by Levine that they would pounce on him, but recommended he go in case they dropped any useful gossip about the show. During the dinner, Downie surreptitiously tied Leigh's shoelaces to the table and attempted to hold him down when he fell over; Nathan-Turner stood

---

61 Marson, *Totally Tasteless*, p173.
62 Marson, *Totally Tasteless*, pp97-99, 104.
63 Marson, *Totally Tasteless*, pp93, 80.
64 Levine, Ian, quoted in Marson, *Totally Tasteless*, p103.

over him unbuckling his belt, at which point Leigh managed to make his escape[65] Nathan-Turner propositioned future Editor-in-Chief of **Blue Peter** Richard Marson in 1983 and belittled him as 'provincial' when he didn't agree to a threesome with him and Downie[66]; a year later, Downie sexually assaulted him in a lift, and left him hiding in the **Doctor Who** production office looking for a weapon to fight him off with[67]. And these weren't aberrations: it was an open secret that Downie would prowl the conventions looking for young fans who would be willing to have sex with him and/or Nathan-Turner, or who could be convinced to put their unwillingness to one side out of embarrassment, fear or gratitude, or for a promise of help in their acting careers, or just to make the Producer of their favourite show happy[68]. When Nathan-Turner finally fell foul of BBC management, it was for none of these things: it was because new Head of Drama, Series and Serials Jonathan Powell had a personal dislike of him and the show he produced[69].

The received wisdom in fandom is that the 1985 hiatus was the death blow for **Doctor Who**, that it wasn't possible for the same people that broke **Doctor Who** to be the ones who fixed it. The show clearly needed an injection of fresh blood if it was going to survive, but the BBC refused to allow Nathan-Turner to move on as he wanted and had no desire to improve **Doctor Who**[70]; their only desire was that Nathan-Turner would continue to drive fans away or else resign, so

---

[65] Marson, *Totally Tasteless*, pp115-16.
[66] Marson, *Totally Tasteless*, p160.
[67] Marson, *Totally Tasteless*, pp161-162.
[68] Marson, *Totally Tasteless*, pp159-78.
[69] Marson, *Totally Tasteless*, p158.
[70] Sandifer, *TARDIS Eruditorum Volume 6*, p522.

they could cancel the show again without as much fuss[71]. But the fact is that even under those circumstances – after a false start – Nathan-Turner did succeed in making **Doctor Who** a completely different show, putting in place the foundations that meant it could be revived nearly 20 years later. There is a desire to give all the credit for that to Andrew Cartmel, but there is no version of the story of the Cartmel era that doesn't have John Nathan-Turner at the heart of it, even if all you credit him with is having the good judgement to hire Cartmel and keep out of his way. John Nathan-Turner should never have been given a position of power in the BBC, but if he hadn't been it is hard to think of any other circumstances in which **Doctor Who** would have continued into the 1980s, let alone come back again.

And that is deeply difficult, because John Nathan-Turner is a deeply difficult figure. There is a desire to solve the problem, to work out which of the conflicting accounts of Nathan-Turner reveals the real man. But that would be a mistake: they all do. John Nathan-Turner was a kind, thoughtful man who would do anything for his friends; he was the life and soul of the party, refusing to let society tell him to tone it down, to shut up and pretend not to be who he was; he was an addict who was enabled by his employer while it suited them and then abandoned when he failed to notice the culture at the BBC changing around him[72]; he was self-important and controlling, bitchy and cruel to anyone he decided didn't deserve his kindness; he was a powerful man who abused his power in ways that would have seen him pulled into #MeToo and Operation Yewtree if he hadn't died when he did.

---

[71] Marson, *Totally Tasteless*, pp194-95.
[72] Marson, *Totally Tasteless*, pp275-78.

Faced with a problem, **Doctor Who** solved it the only way it could: in the metatext. All of the problems facing **Doctor Who** at the time found their way into the story, including Nathan-Turner: to the BBC – and to Nathan-Turner himself – **Doctor Who** was the Producer and the Producer was **Doctor Who**. *The Greatest Show* made Nathan-Turner the Circus, the camp entertainment trying to soldier on despite a drastic change in its fortunes. One that hid dark secrets and abuses of power that hurt, amongst others, the very fans it inspired. This isn't to say that this metatextual smuggling was a deliberate, conscious act, or to suggest that anyone was complicit in the abuse taking place. Wyatt has since written *Me and Him and Who* (2022) about this very subject, but:

> '...at the time of writing *Greatest Show* I knew very little about JNT and Gary's behaviour with the fans: the central part of your thesis is one I really don't accept. It certainly never occurred to me that the Psychic Circus was any sort of analogy for their behaviour.'[73]

But since Roland Barthes' *The Death of the Author* (1967), we know that authorial intent isn't the only meaning that a story has, and now – with nearly 40 years of hindsight – it's hard to argue that *The Greatest Show* hasn't developed a greater meaning. Over four episodes, it shows that this Doctor and his new companion Ace could face every problem down – both within and without the story – and walk away from the explosion without even looking back. More than any other story in the Cartmel era, *The Greatest Show* is a clear statement of intent about what the production team planned to do, an acknowledgement that what had gone before wouldn't work for

---

[73] Stephen Wyatt, author's own interview.

this new era, but could be built and rebuilt to provide the foundations for a new Circus. One that, if nothing else, would be worth watching.

TEARS OF A CLOWN

In the beginning, John Nathan-Turner wanted to record a story at Longleat, Wiltshire, which was home to a safari park, the largest hedge maze in the world and – more relevantly – BBC Enterprise's Doctor Who Exhibition. This evolved into a story set in a circus through discussion with Stephen Wyatt and Andrew Cartmel[74], who was less than impressed with the original idea:

> 'I couldn't imagine a worse location [than a fairground]. It was so trite and kitsch and boring. [...] But halfway through the meeting, which proved to be a rather dead end discussion, John suddenly said, of his own volition, "I'm going off the idea as we talk about it".'[75]

A circus proved to be a much more fertile ground: Cartmel was keen for a story that reflected the mood of *The Circus of Doctor Lao* (1935) but – despite Tat Wood identifying *The Greatest Show* as 'plundered wholesale' from the book – Stephen Wyatt was less keen and quickly dismissed it[76]. Instead, he set about developing the Psychic Circus as a metaphor made manifest – 'Two realities – the apparent and the one underneath'[77] – which gradually developed, as we have seen, into a commentary on the state of **Doctor Who** as a whole at the time.

---

[74] *The Complete History*, p56.
[75] Cartmel, *Script Doctor*, p132.
[76] Wood, *About Time 6*, p709; Cartmel, *Script Doctor*, p133.
[77] Wyatt's original story outline, quoted in Griffiths, 'Honk, the Squonk and a Green Non-Entity'.

It wasn't the first time that clowns had appeared in **Doctor Who**, with Joey and Clara featuring in *The Celestial Toymaker* (1966), the Doctor's brief vision of his reflection as a laughing clown in *The Deadly Assassin* (1976), Dukkha in *Kinda* (1982) generating the same sense of unease that the Chief Clown does with his pale face and leering grin. Nor was it the last: an ex-guest of *The God Complex* (2011) had a mortal terror of clowns that caused one to appear briefly. The Chief Clown is, however, the first – and to date only – time that clowns have been the main antagonists in a television **Doctor Who** story, which feels like somebody had been missing the obvious, considering coulrophobia is one of the most well-known phobias[78] and **Doctor Who** had always had a penchant for terrifying its viewers.

Coulrophobia may be well known, but it is in its own way mysterious. To begin with, nobody really knows where the term comes from: it was first used sometime in 1987 and appears to be a nonsense word, with the prefix being neither Greek nor Latin and having no clear meaning[79]. Most dictionaries give the derivation as **kōlobathristés** – stilt walkers – but given that words for clowns do exist in Ancient Greek, the suggestion that the word is mistakenly using the Modern Greek **klooun** seems the more convincing[80]. The term is completely absent from *The Encyclopedia of Phobias, Fears, and Anxieties* (1989),

---

[78] Summerscale, Kate, 'Top 10 Phobias and What They Reveal About the Strangeness of Life'.

[79] Langley, Travis. 'The Lost Origin of Coulrophobia, the Abnormal Fear of Clowns'.

[80] *Online Etymology Dictionary*, 'coulrophobia (n.)'.

which probably explains why there is no explanatory comment from the Doctor about the scientific term for Ace's fear.

Except that Ace doesn't suffer from coulrophobia and neither do many others: a phobia is a medically diagnosed mental condition that requires a significant impact on an individual's health and happiness, with the kind of general uneasiness that Ace and many others show towards clowns not qualifying[81]. In truth, even that isn't so common: research into clowns in a clinical setting carried out across Europe has shown that only a very small proportion of children report unease around them[82].

But this unease seems to be the effect Wyatt wants his clowns to have. They – and particularly the Chief Clown – are a good fit with the story, thematically: the most famous clown in the world remains Ronald McDonald [83], to the point where he has also become synonymous with the various failings of large corporations – or, for our purposes, the 60s generation's celebrating of things that the 80s generation saw as unacceptable. In 1986, 'London Greenpeace' targeted a number of demonstrations against McDonalds, which may possibly have put the idea of Ronald McDonald – always a slightly creepy clown, particularly in his first Willard Scott incarnation – into Wyatt's mind[84]. They also fit into the metatext we have identified in *The Greatest Show*: as a character who was a talented and

---

[81] Langley, 'The Lost Origin of Coulrophobia'.

[82] Radford, Benjamin, *Bad Clowns*, p38.

[83] Which means that the Chief Clown could be seen as **Doctor Who** appropriating a corporate emblem and transforming it into a source of horror for a generation of children: a close – although less visually obvious – cousin to the Kandyman in *The Happiness Patrol* (1988).

[84] Radford, *Bad Clowns*, pp127-29.

enthusiastic participant in the success of the Psychic Circus, but is now hiding sinister truths behind a smile as he carries out the instructions of the Gods above him, there is more than a hint of John Nathan-Turner about the Chief Clown. But more than anything, the clowns' role in the story is that of the traditional monster, with the audience expected to share Ace's assessment of them as 'creepy'. With the addition of Ian Reddington's much better than strictly required performance, the Chief Clown is elevated into the ranks of the great **Doctor Who** monsters, which is impressive given that he achieves his status with little more than some face paint and the most unsettling wave ever committed to television.

That face paint marks the Chief Clown out as a Pierrot, his look most probably inspired by David Bowie's turn as one in his video for 'Ashes to Ashes' (1980): the song alludes in part to Bowie's Major Tom character (from 'Space Oddity' (1969)) having moved from hero to junkie, and reflects a similar theme of the Hippy Generation losing their way in the 80s[85]. But Pierrot has much longer history than that, coming from the improvised Commedia dell'Arte, the earliest professional secular theatre in Europe and an influence on Shakespeare and Molière, and 'possibly the most revolutionary development in the history of European theatre' between the 16th and 18th centuries'[86].

The Commedia probably developed from earlier Greek and Roman theatre[87] – although it may equally have been influenced by Eastern

---

[85] Stevens and Moore, '47 Cool Things'.
[86] Jordan, Peter, 'In Search of Pantalone and the Origins of the Commedia dell'Arte'.
[87] Jordan, 'In Search of Pantalone'.

theatrical forms introduced to Italy by earlier trade with China, Japan and India[88] – but introduced its own innovations, not least of which was being the first theatrical form to use real women as performers. Whilst improvised – although there is still debate about just how much – the Commedia relied on stock characters based on the popular stereotypes of the regions and cities of Italy and the different classes that inhabited them: Pantalone the ancient Venetian merchant[89]; Il Dottore (pleasingly for us, 'the Doctor'), the Bolognese pompous professional who is overly fond of the sound of his own voice (so probably the Third Il Dottore, then); and of course Pierrot, the servant, the sad clown with the white face make-up who pines for his unrequited love Columbine[90].

Pierrot is one of the few characters in the Commedia to go unmasked, allowing the audience to truly feel his pain as his unrequited love pairs off with fellow clown Harlequin. And he does evoke sympathy, because the zanni[91] of the Commedia aren't clowns in the modern sense of the word: it is only relatively recently that clowns became associated with children's entertainment, and they have a much longer history as a theatrical tradition. The clowns of the Commedia are comedic, yes: Harlequin, the brightly coloured clown, was a trickster figure related to the medieval jester (and the source of the costume worn by the Doctor in *Black Orchid* (1982)) and Pulcinella, the opportunistic bumpkin who always takes the winning side. But

---

[88] Fulchignoni, Enrico, 'Oriental Influences on the Commedia dell'Arte'.
[89] Jordan, 'In Search of Pantalone'.
[90] Ars Comica, 'THE COMMEDIA MUST GO ON'.
[91] The name for the clown characters in the Commedia is also where English gets the word 'zany' from.

every time a modern clown appeals to pathos or inspires sympathy from the crowd, it is Pierrot they are invoking.

This inner sadness behind the painted smile – the so-called Tears of a Clown – has long been associated with clowning in the UK, and has an unlikely godfather: Charles Dickens, who edited the biography of the first of the modern clowns, Joseph Grimaldi. Grimaldi's breakout role was as Clown in Thomas Dibdin and Charles Farley's *Harlequin and Mother Goose; or, the Golden Egg* in 1806, and he went on to be seen by an estimated eighth of the population of London every year. Grimaldi took the more stylised and minimalist clowns of the day and revitalised them, adding bright wigs, large ruffs and eye-catching make-up to create the clown he called Joey: you will be familiar with what Joey looks like, because the costume and make-up is the kind worn by the robot clowns in *The Greatest Show*, and this type of clown is still called a Joey today.

But Grimaldi suffered from crushing depression – he is the inspiration for the joke where a depressed patient is prescribed a trip to see a famous clown, only to tell his doctor 'but I'm that clown!' – and also a number of physical complaints so exacerbated by his performances that he ended up retiring at the age of 42[92]. At his retirement performance, Grimaldi could barely manage a few songs, and announced that he was 'sinking fast'. After his death, Dickens was called in to reorganise Grimaldi's autobiography for publication, but his own suspicion of theatricality and performance as an 'inherently destructive endeavor' primed him to draw out the tragedy of Grimaldi's story – the broken clown hiding his true self

---

[92] By contrast, Grimaldi's father was also a clown who went on performing well into his 70s.

behind the white make-up – and seed the popular belief that clowns are fundamentally pretending to be something they are not, and so untrustworthy[93].

But if Grimaldi and Pierrot convinced people that clowns were secretly sad, some of Pierrot's fellow zanni convinced the public that there was far worse going on.

The Commedia was being performed in England by at least the 1540s, and were being imitated by English writers and performers almost immediately. By the early 1720s, these imitations had settled into a more structured performance, the pantomime: as with clowning, this was different to the modern pantomime that developed from it, but similarities and connective tissue remained. The traditional pantomime was structured in two halves, with the first 'serious' half usually drawn from mythology and a second 'comic' or 'grotesque' part that centred on the antics of Harlequin as he tried to wrest Columbine from the arms of her husband or father, usually a representation of Pantolone or Il Dottore[94]. Harlequin himself was descended from a spectre or demon linked to the Wild Hunt[95], and was a master of trickery, able to transform himself and others to

---

[93] McConnell Stott, Andrew, 'Clowns on the Verge of a Nervous Breakdown: Dickens, Coulrophobia, and the Memoirs of Joseph Grimaldi', *Journal for Early Modern Cultural Studies* Vol 12, No 4, Fall 2012.
[94] O'Brien, John, 'Harlequin Britain: Eighteenth-Century Pantomime and the Cultural Location of Entertainment(s)', *Theatre Journal* Vol 50, No 4, December 1998.
[95] Radford, *Bad Clowns*, p6.

achieve his ends. And he carried out his machinations in complete silence, as dictated by the 'mime' in 'pantomime'.

By the time Garrick produced *Harlequin's Invasion* in 1759, Harlequin – already linked by history to the ancient enemy France – was being symbolically chased from the stage by the more legitimate English theatre of Shakespeare (represented by a statue that loomed up to frighten the vagabond Harlequin away at the end of the Harlequinade section), and when Grimaldi died, pantomime was already considered a thing of the past, something both decadent and frivolous that wouldn't be missed[96].

Worse was what Pulcinella got up to. Harlequin couldn't be trusted but was merely a trickster, not actively evil; Pulcinella came to England and committed repeated murders, killing his wife and their baby and the policeman who came to arrest him. He was sentenced to hang but escaped the noose only to be claimed by the Devil himself. Pulcinella also had a history that went beyond the Commedia, and he was the star of Italian puppet shows, where his hunchback and hook nose were exaggerated to the point of terror. On 9 May 1662, he appeared at Covent Garden in an Anglicised version of one of these puppet shows, rechristened Punch and paired with his long-suffering wife and victim Judy. And unlike Harlequin, he was given a voice – a strange, inhuman cackle produced using a tool called a swazzle or swatchel: his cry of 'That's the way to do it!' has echoed down the centuries, and still receives

---

[96] O'Brien, 'Harlequin Britain'; McConnell Stott, 'Clowns on the Verge of a Nervous Breakdown'.

condemnation today as being unsuitable entertainment for young children[97].

Uneasiness around clowns was well established in the English-speaking world and survived all the way through to the production of *The Greatest Show*. In 1981, the fear of clowns was still strong enough to fuel rumours that gangs of clowns were abducting or molesting children in Massachusetts: the so-called phantom clowns were never seen by an adult witness, but this didn't stop further panics breaking out again in 1982, and spreading across America in the early 1980s[98]. As late as 2016, another wave of homicidal clown sightings swept across the world – possibly inspired by the news that another film based on Stephen King's *It* (1986) was in production, or folk memories of the 1980s outbreak – but in at least one state of America, investigating police discovered that there was no evidence that the clowns themselves had ever existed[99].

However, in 2013 the phantom clown made it into the real world: in Northampton, England, reports started coming in about a clown wandering the streets in silence and creeping people out. A Facebook page quickly sprang up to track the clown's movements, and he was eventually unmasked as a prankster. Whilst the Northampton Clown was friendly enough – often stopping to allow people to take pictures of or even with him – and he was never

---

[97] Radford, *Bad Clowns*, pp11-19, although some of the more modern instances of this moral panic have the hallmarks of a 'They're trying to ban Christmas now!' tabloid invention.
[98] Radford, *Bad Clowns*, pp151-58.
[99] Romano, Aja, 'The Great Clown Panic of 2016 is a Hoax. But the Terrifying Side of Clowns is Real.'

treated as a serious threat, his incongruous appearance and complete silence had a big impact on the people of Northampton: he received thousands of death threats, and was threatened in the street by a man with a knife. He also inspired several copycat clowns: whilst these early clown sightings were innocent jokes, by the time the phenomenon reached France, things had developed and clowns were being seen carrying real weapons, and in some cases criminals dressed as clowns in an attempt to disappear into the general panic over scary clowns attacking people[100].

The BBC weren't unaware of the power of the scary clown. In 1985, they broadcast a programme called **The Golden Oldie Picture Show** (1985-88), the conceit of which was modern directors creating music videos for songs too old to have them: the last episode of the first series, broadcast on 13 January 1985, included Manfred Mann's 'Ha Ha Said The Clown' (1968) which featured a decidedly creepy clown with an exaggerated rubber nose, leering out of a series of frames directly at the viewer. Whilst this clown is a clear ancestor of the Chief Clown, it wasn't him or any of the other clowns that Wyatt was inspired by – indeed, the unease around clowns that he was channelling was his own:

> 'The Chief Clown's look was inspired by my childhood visits to the Circus. I was fascinated by these tall graceful white face clowns in beautiful glittery costumes who never got involved in messy slapstick like the 'ordinary' clowns did. And yes, they were scary.'[101]

---

[100] Radford, *Bad Clowns*, pp99-106.
[101] Stephen Wyatt, author's own interview.

By including the clowns, he was trying to solve two problems in one: the need for a monster, and the need for it to be both practical and frightening:

> 'I'd always felt that, by and large, monsters don't work very well on **Doctor Who**, and monsters on location largely consisted of rather embarrassed actors in silly costumes wishing they were dead! [T]he robotic clowns were one of my solutions to the problem. They could all look the same, and that was quite scary in itself. Every time the clowns were in the scene it made it better.'[102]

Ian Reddington's Chief Clown was so effectively creepy in his costume and make-up, it was decided to use casts of his face as the masks for the robot clowns, which gave them an additional uniformity on top of that afforded by their makeup[103]. That makeup – since the days of Grimaldi – frequently emphasises and duplicates the features of a normal human face: eyes, eyebrows, rosy cheeks and a fixed and constant smile. This can evoke the psychological effect called 'the uncanny', whereby something is at once familiar and disturbingly strange at the same time: clowns can seem to all have one face – quite literally, in the case of The Greatest Show – that they use to disguise their true face. We sense that they are human but not-human, replaying on a smaller scale the story of contact with the other that is SF's main legacy of its colonial past[104]. We know that clowns' smiling faces are just a mask, and could be hiding any

---

[102] Wyatt in Griffiths, 'Oh What a Circus'.

[103] Cartmel, Script Doctor, p138.

[104] Radford, 'Bad Clowns', pp20-22; Rieder, John, Colonialism and the Emergence of Science Fiction, p77.

number of sinister intentions: a fear described by author Robert Bloch as 'the fear of a human being who doesn't look, think or act like a human being'. Worse, we know that the clown exists outside our usual social norms and frequently interact with others in strange and unusual ways: often this is with other clowns and we can convince ourselves that we are safe from their attention, but to meet a clown on its own is to become part of their performance, for better or, God help us, for worse[105].

> This is part of the toolkit of the scary clown: clowns in the ring of a circus are in their proper context. Take a clown anywhere else and that context is broken, their behaviour suddenly inexplicable and unnerving. The actor Lon Chaney Snr expressed the same concern: 'A clown is funny in the circus ring, but what would be the normal reaction to opening a door at midnight and finding the same clown there in the moonlight?'[106]

This juxtaposition and context stripping is used in *The Greatest Show* to immediately unsettle the audience, giving us brightly painted clowns driving across the sand dunes of an alien world in a black hearse, with no diegetic explanation ever being given for their choice of transportation. It is part of the layers of Reddington's performance, with the Chief Clown having a different voice when he is on stage or performing than when he thinks he is not being watched by his audience. He is a different person when in context, brighter and more traditionally clown-like, than when he is out of context. This is reflected in the behaviour of the robot clowns, who on stage appear

---

[105] Radford, *Bad Clowns*, pp20-22.
[106] Lon Chaney Snr, quoted in Radford, *Bad Clowns*, p20.

completely human, but could just as easily be deactivated, dismembered and waiting to kill their creator in a darkened workshop.

Many histories will tell you that the scary clown is a modern phenomenon, pushed into the mainstream by stories of clown and serial killer John Wayne Gacy, arrested at the end of 1978[107]. However, Gacy was a killer who occasionally dressed as a clown when volunteering at parties, and never during his attacks, and his notoriety was always greater in his native United States than it was elsewhere, which makes him an unlikely patient zero for an epidemic[108]. In truth, it is possible to identify more scary clowns in the media today than there were in the past; but there is also more media, and the boundaries of what is acceptable have also expanded since the early days of film. There is no evidence that fear of clowns has increased since the 1980s, because there is no reliable evidence of how afraid of clowns people were before that[109]. But, as Lon Chaney Snr tells us, at least one person found them unsettling before Gacy was even born: his quote was probably given during publicity for one of two scary clown films he made in the 1920s – *He Who Gets Slapped* (1924) *and Laugh Clown Laugh* (1928) – which both feature circus clowns driven mad by love[110].

---

[107] Silman, Jon, 'How Did John Wayne Gacy Fit into The Origin Of The "Evil Clown"?' See, for instance, Rodriguez McRobbie, Linda, 'The History and Psychology of Clowns Being Scary' and BBC News, 'Creepy Clown Craze: How Dangerous Are Clowns Really?'.
[108] Chaney Snr quoted in Radford, *Bad Clowns*, pp111-13.
[109] Radford, *Bad Clowns*, pp32-33.
[110] Radford, *Bad Clowns*, pp52-53.

Certainly, the most famous example of the scary clown predates Gacy by a long way: Batman's clown-faced antagonist the Joker is nearly as old as Batman, debuting in the first issue of **Batman** on 25 April 1940. He was based on a character played by Conrad Veidt in *The Man Who Laughs* (1928), the man in question being Gwynplaine, who has been surgically mutilated to always have a fixed grin[111]. Inspired by a photograph of Veidt in character from the film, Bob Kane, Jerry Robinson and Bill Finger created a sadistic serial killer who left victims sporting a similar rictus grin.

Along with Gacy, the other clown most likely to be mentioned as being the first scary clown is Pennywise the dancing clown[112]. He was a supernatural force of evil created by Stephen King after he asked himself the question 'What scares children more than anything else in the world?' and got the answer 'Clowns' [113]. King was an established writer of horror stories, and when Pennywise appeared in *It* (1986), a new Stephen King novel was a big deal. However, Pennywise didn't become what he is today until the ABC network broadcast a two-part adaptation of the novel in 1990 starring Tim Curry: because the adaptation was broadcast on television, it didn't

---

[111] Whilst Gwynplaine is not specifically a clown, his grin and his occupation acting in a travelling show mark him out as another early antecedent.
[112] Tikkanen, Amy, '10 Famous Clowns: From Comical to Creepy'; Marshall, Rick, 'No Laughing Matter: The Scariest Clowns From Movies and TV'; Luiz, HC, 'Top Secret Clown Business: Six of the Scariest Clowns in Horror Movies'.
[113] Radford, *Bad Clowns*, pp67-68.

require a film classification, which would have cut its audience significantly[114].

The same can be said of the Joker, who gained increased worldwide notoriety when Jack Nicholson played him in Tim Burton's *Batman* (1989)[115], albeit too late to be a direct influence on *The Greatest Show*, for which Wyatt delivered his final scripts on 8 January 1988[116]. There were other films – the cult classic *Killer Klowns from Outer Space* (1988), or *Blood Harvest* (1987), for example – and a rock band called Wall of Voodoo, who released a video for 'Far Side of Crazy' in 1985 that featured a scary clown[117]. Pleasingly – given the presence of the Ringmaster in *The Greatest Show* – even Flavor Flav of Public Enemy, who released their first album in 1987, has been described as 'a clown with consciousness' because of the traits he shares with traditional clowns: rebellious behaviour, comic pratfalls and oversized clothing accessories[118]. It is unlikely that any of these were a direct influence on *The Greatest Show* – certainly, Wyatt was unaware of It[119] – but these clowns either originating or gaining high-profile incarnations in the decade after Gacy's arrest does add weight to the suggestion that scary clowns were part of the zeitgeist of the 1980s.

But *The Greatest Show* does something that is atypical for the period. Most of the scary clowns around in the 80s use gore as part of the

---

[114] Radford, *Bad Clowns*, pp67-69.
[115].
[116] Radford, *Bad Clowns*, pp63-65; Molesworth, *John Nathan-Turner Production Diary'*, p353.
[117] Radford, *Bad Clowns*, pp 54, 75, 78.
[118] Radford, *Bad Clowns*, p85.
[119] Stephen Wyatt, author's own interview.

effect of their scariness: Pennywise kills a boy by pulling his arm off and later stands smiling and waving the dismembered limb at the boy's brother; the Joker uses physical violence and disfigurement as a calling card; one of the Killer Klowns uses a dead policeman as a ventriloquist dummy. The Chief Clown avoids this tactic, for the obvious reason that the BBC still considered **Doctor Who** to be a children's show that inexplicably attracted an adult audience.

Instead, Reddington gives a performance that relies almost exclusively on using the disconnect between his physical appearance and his actual role in the story to unsettle the audience. He is sinister. What he shows is that clowns are a powerful image in and of themselves, and even without explicit gore they can have a deeply unnerving effect on people. And that is the way that Wyatt and Cartmel use the clowns in *The Greatest Show*, in accordance with a wider desire to have the audience reconnect with **Doctor Who** by focussing it more on the characters. It's a shift from the Saward era of the show, where many of the characters were hardbitten mercenaries and/or just unlikeable, and the monsters were frightening because they killed a lot of people. By contrast, the clowns themselves don't kill many people, but we know that they are scary because Ace is afraid of them.

This is quite a rare situation in **Doctor Who**: companions aren't generally scared of the monsters, except when they are being directly threatened by them. If they are shown to have a prejudice against someone or something, they have usually resolved it by the end of the story. But in *The Greatest Show*, Ace is creeped out by the clowns before she or the Doctor discover there is anything untoward happening on Segonax, and by the end of the story her irrational fear has been rationalised: the clowns **were** sinister and dangerous, and she was right to be afraid of them.

This means of course that the traditional way of looking at what the Doctor is doing in *The Greatest Show* is wrong: it is frequently said that the Doctor is helping Ace to overcome her fear of clowns, but that clearly isn't true. What Ace actually learns in *The Greatest Show* is that clowns are scary, just as she learns in *Ghost Light* that she was right to be afraid in Gabriel Chase. Rather than teaching her to face her fears, the Doctor appears to be teaching Ace that she has good instincts and she shouldn't feel bad about trusting them.

But that isn't all that she sees in *The Greatest Show*: she also sees a lot of rebellion. Bellboy, Flower-Child and Deadbeat rebel against the Gods of Ragnarok, despite – certainly in Deadbeat's case – having been previously more than happy to side with them, and despite previous disobedience having cost them dear. Mags rebelling against Captain Cook is perhaps most significant, however, given that it occurs within the pseudo-Doctor and companion team that the story has set up, and that Mags is so closely tied to Ace. She sees a companion turn on her Doctor because he has gone too far, because too many people have been hurt and someone needs to protect those that are left. The production team at the time were toying with the idea that the Doctor was testing Ace, helping her to grow so that she could enrol at the Academy on Gallifrey and become a Time Lord[120], but what *The Greatest Show* implies is perhaps the more

---

[120] Sullivan, Shannon, '**Doctor Who**: The Lost Stories (The Seventh Doctor)'.

dramatic storyline: that the Doctor is testing Ace because one day he will go too far, and he will need her to stand up to him.

This is the reason for the Doctor travelling with companions that Russell T Davies explicitly wrote into stories like *The Runaway Bride* (2006) and *Turn Left* (2008), and with hindsight we can see the seeds of it here in *The Greatest Show*. The story reaches out into the future and impossibly grabs hold of one of the main ideas of the revived series. It knows the end is coming, but it looks towards a future where it can come back and thrive again.

LET THERE BE ROCK

Across all of its genre productions, there is nothing that the BBC likes more than a quarry: the idea that if you operate a quarry in the UK, at some point the BBC will turn up wanting to use it as the Planet Zog or the Desert of Eternal Despair is so ingrained in the British psyche that it has evolved into a trope[121]. Quarries were useful because, as well as looking roughly like what audiences had come to expect for the surface of alien bodies from pictures of the moon and Mars, they were usually below the level of the surrounding area and so any buildings or other signs of human life were safely hidden out of shot. But so often was the quarry used as a cheap stand-in for alien worlds, the practice very quickly became cliche, a symbol of cheapness or a lack of imagination, and many people involved in the production of **Doctor Who** wanted to avoid them at all costs:

> 'I'd said to Alan Wareing at the beginning 'we mustn't have the gravel pit. Please not the **Doctor Who** gravel pit!' And though in effect we got a quarry, he chose it because it had a slightly different feel, with little pools of water.'[122]

This view of quarries is certainly reflected in Cartmel's era on the show: outside of season 24 – where one story featured three separate quarries but Cartmel had limited ability to course-correct – only three stories featured quarries, and only two used them as alien planets[123]. Of those two stories – *The Greatest Show* and *Survival* –

---

[121] TV tropes, 'BBC Quarry'.

[122] Wyatt in Griffiths, 'Oh What a Circus Oh What a Show'.

[123] *Doctor Who Locations Guide*, 'Season Twenty-Four', 'Season Twenty-Five', 'Season Twenty-Six'. The third was *Battlefield* (1989), which used the Castle Cement Quarry in Kettleton for pyrotechnics

both used Warmwell Quarry in Dorset. Part of this was the simple reason that only these two stories featured any significant time spent on alien worlds, as Cartmel's realisation that the BBC could do period drama very well led him to move the show to more Earthly settings. But that shift didn't result in **Doctor Who** becoming completely studio-based: the production team settled into alternating between studio-based and location-based stories for the rest of their run, with *The Greatest Show* being intended to be studio-based until circumstances forced a rethink.

One of the reasons that some locations get reused is purely practical: since the enclosure of the commons[124] introduced absolute private ownership of land, a complex web of companies and shell companies has grown up holding ownership of every location in the UK. Production crews must obtain filming permission from the land owner before location shooting can begin, but finding out who actually owns a piece of land and getting them to respond in time can be increasingly difficult: in practice, a handful of locations across the UK with sympathetic and above all identifiable owners tend to stand in for a lot of the world[125]. Another is cost: **Doctor Who** was seen within the BBC as something of a curate's egg, a children's show that had ideas above its station. As such, the budget the BBC grudgingly gave it was always less that it needed – the BBC were

---

work when Ancelyn crashes into a hill on arrival, presumably on the grounds that quarries are less concerned about things blowing up than Rutland Water.

[124] A series of United Kingdom Acts of Parliament which enclosed 6.8 million acres of open fields and common land between 1604 and 1914.

[125] *Mandatory Redistribution Party*, 'Moon Hermit | 046'.

reluctant to allow the show to go far past *An Unearthly Child* (1963) because of an overspend on its original budget, mostly caused by the TARDIS set – and the BBC's brightest and best usually tried to avoid it[126]. Studio work and quarries were all that the show could afford[127].

Location shooting does have its advantages over studio filming: it is harder to control lighting and sound, but by removing the need to build every item that is going to be seen on screen it can be more economical, especially if you tend towards cheaper locations like quarries over more expensive and difficult ones like stately homes or central London. It is also a lot easier to make a location appear real on camera than a studio, as anyone who has watched **Doctor Who**'s wide collection of polystyrene rocks bouncing around the screen can attest.

It can also be something of a perk of the job, not just for the cast who get to go somewhere new and hang out together in the hotel bar, but for the member of the production team that goes to do the initial 'recce' of a potential location: it seems unlikely that it was coincidence that it was Gary Downie and/or John Nathan-Turner who got to scout locations in Spain, Amsterdam and Lanzarote. And if you went somewhere particularly exciting, it could also drum up a bit of extra publicity. For **Doctor Who**, though, the main advantage of a good location shoot was that it could get you a vaguely realistic-looking alien planet, especially if you found yourself a nice, cheap quarry.

---

[126] Marson, *Totally Tasteless*, pp70-71; Hadoke, Toby, *Doctor Who: Toby Hadoke's Time Travels*.
[127] Marson, *Totally Tasteless*, p71.

In some ways, however, **Doctor Who** was getting it right. When *The Greatest Show* was being made, the production team only had the planets of our solar system to use as a guide, and from that evidence it seemed that rocky planets were the most likely to form: Mercury, Venus, Earth, and Mars are all 'terrestrial' planets formed of rock, with Jupiter and Saturn being 'gas giants' and Uranus and Neptune being 'Neptunian', i.e. with a rocky core, but mostly made of various kinds of gases[128]. At that point, Pluto was still considered a planet and again was rocky[129]. Since then, however, thousands of planets have been discovered outside our solar system by careful measurement of the behaviour of stars, and NASA keep a running total on their website, which at point of writing has 5,272 confirmed exoplanets found and the most prevalent being Neptunian, at 1,834 to 'terrestrial' and 'super-Earth's 1,797[130]. Thus we see the dangers of basis a hypothesis on too small a sample size: if Cartmel and his colleagues had wanted to show a truly realistic alien world, they should have tried a location shoot inside a freezing hydrogen chamber.

But this is **Doctor Who**, and **Doctor Who** is very, very rarely hard SF; it isn't interested in presenting a realistic version of alien worlds. Instead, it uses its locations for their impact on the viewer, usually in very broad brush strokes: the rural settings seen in stories like *Spearhead From Space* (1970) and *The Android Invasion* (1975) are shorthand for safe normality that can then be disrupted by the arrival

---

[128] NASA, 'What Is An Exoplanet?'.
[129] NASA, 'Planets'. There is also a potential 'Planet X', which since Pluto's downgrading is now disappointingly called the Ninth Planet and does not appear to be a mirror image of Earth.
[130] NASA. 'Exoplanets'.

of the alien and strange; the Victoriana of *The Talons of Weng-Chiang* (1977) and *Ghost Light* is a shorthand for 'the past'; the quarries of *Destiny of the Daleks* (1979) or *Time and the Rani* (1987) a quick way to suggest that the Doctor is somewhere unfamiliar where danger could lurk around any corner. They aren't intended to teach us anything about alien worlds, or rural villages for that matter: they are there to give us pre-warning of what kind of story we are going to see this week.

What we see in *The Greatest Show* – and more explicitly later in *Survival* – is something slightly different. These stories made use of the 'slightly different feel' of Warmwell Quarry, not entirely as a standard 'alien' backdrop that suggests a sense of not-Earth to the viewer, but specifically as planets that are corrupted and in the process of dying. When the Doctor first arrives on Segonax, he comments that it is 'not quite the green and pleasant land we'd been led to expect', and the implication is that the change has occurred since the Circus stopped travelling and settled down on the 'dreadful place'[131]. When Cartmel allows quarries to be used in his era, he makes them part of the story, an additional character that has information to share: Segonax is a planet that has been corrupted by the Gods of Ragnarok and lost all its former glory; it is the physical representation of the Gods' power to destroy, the same story beat as Bellboy and Deadbeat saying the Chief Clown used to be funny and inventive before he became the Gods' henchman. The idea that places can have meaning beyond just being a collection of physical characteristics has long been understood, and was named

---

[131] Part One.

psychogeography by French philosopher Guy Debord in 1955. As the writer Alan Moore puts it:

> 'Psychogeography would be the understanding that in our experience of any place, it is the associations, the dreams, the imaginings, the history – it is all the information that is relevant to that place which is what we experience when we talk about a place [...] That is psychogeography – a way of considering the landscape around us as more than its physical components.'[132]

It has often been remarked that Cartmel's stated desire taking the job as **Doctor Who** Script Editor was to 'bring down the government'[133], and that is an ambition he shares with probably the most famous work of psychogeography, Alan Moore's *From Hell* (1989-98). In *From Hell*, Moore presents what is ostensibly just one more in a long list of theories of who Jack the Ripper really was, settling on royal physician Sir William Gull. But Moore gives us clues that there is more to his story than that right from the start: Gull had been widely discredited as a possible suspect for the Ripper when Moore started writing, mostly because he was 71 and barely recovered from a serious stroke when the murders occurred, and Moore's title comes from the 'From Hell' letter delivered to the chairman of the Whitechapel Vigilance Committee and also most

---

[132] Moore in Vollmar, Rob, 'Northampton Calling: A Conversation with Alan Moore'.
[133] Sylvester McCoy in Cartmel, *Script Doctor*, p15.

likely a hoax[134]. Moore even undermines one of the linchpins of the theory he is detailing, having the person responsible for first identifying Gull as the Ripper admit that he was making it up[135]. While the trappings of a Ripper Theory are there in *From Hell* – Gull is ostensibly carrying out the murders to cover up a scandal involving the Duke of Clarence – even Gull himself is at one step remove from them: his own motive is the completion of a psychogeographical journey that will allow him to transcend history and become as a god.

There are multiple interpretations of what *From Hell* is really about, but Ann Tso in *The Literary London Journal* focuses on Gull's journeying across London to form hers. She suggests that:

> 'Gull sees London as the microcosmic representation of his country, his England, and thus of "Englishness"—the culmination of English history, as it were. He reads Londonscape to trace Englishness, which, he assumes, should unite the London community and thereby define London.'

In a perversion of the more standard definition of psychogeography, Gull's journey to the sites of specific events in English history, and his feelings towards them, calls forth a unified sense of English exceptionalism that he hopes will become true for all time. He seeks narrative closure, the end of the story of England where the final line will always be that she was greatest. In giving Gull this grand

---

[134] Hussey, Dr Kristin. '"Fools and Savages Explain: Wise Men Investigate" Sir William Withey Gull'; Margaritoff, Marco, 'Jack The Ripper's "From Hell" Letter and the Macabre Story Behind It'.
[135] Carpenter, Greg, *The British Invasion: Alan Moore, Neil Gaiman, Grant Morrison, and the Invention of the Modern Comic Book Writer*, p176.

endeavour, Moore is directly paralleling the politics of the time; Thatcher was also undertaking a similar endeavour, remembering her version of the greatness of the Victorian era that was Gull's present and mapping it onto her own present with calls to revive 'Victorian values' of self-reliance, morality and duty, plus a healthy amount of nationalism to give it more flavour. And in this shared endeavour, Gull at least seems able to claim some success: with each murder he is afforded glimpses of the future, until at the close of the story he ascends through history to come to Moore's present day.

But Moore's choice to make this story, about Thatcher's efforts to define the English character by evoking the Victorian past, a Jack the Ripper story is both deliberate and inspired. The very existence of psychogeography shows that there can be no such thing as a unified experience of place or time – that is why Gull's version of psychogeography is a perversion. That it is Jack the Ripper who tries to define the notion of English exceptionalism only serves to undermine it: the Ripper demonstrates none of the supposed virtues of the Victorian era, and builds his vision of the future on the mutilated bodies of murdered women. And yet he has become one of the cornerstones of the modern notion of the age, alongside the work of Dickens and Conan Doyle, the snow and the fog. Any definition of English superiority that includes the Ripper is doomed to be self-defeating: as Gull ascends through history, he suddenly finds himself descending again to the 19th century, where a woman with four children named for Gull's victims tells him to 'clear off back to hell and leave us be'. Gull realises that 'all things at the last are sullied', and disappears from the story[136].

The psychogeography in *The Greatest Show* can be seen to be working in the same way, although to a different end. *From Hell* is Gull's psychogeographical journey, forcing his opinions of the landscape and history onto the world around him, and *The Greatest Show* is Ace's; she arrives on Segonax with the Doctor doing his best to convince her that the locals are friendly and all that will happen is an entertaining time at the Circus, but as she journeys towards the big top, her own fears and misgivings imprint themselves on the landscape around her. The road is barren and dusty, nothing grows, and sustenance is foul-tasting and only available in exchange for money. There are dangers literally buried under the sand, dangers that can and do rise up unexpectedly to do them harm. The Circus is a bright painted smile on a cold emotionless face, her fear of clowns made manifest. If Gull's journey seeks to impose closure on the notion of English history, Ace's conversely seeks to avoid it: by imposing hidden dangers and sinister intentions on the landscape, Ace injects drama where none would otherwise exist, and keeps the story of **Doctor Who** moving forward for three more episodes. This is one of the roles that the post-2005 series has suggested the companions play: allowing the Doctor to keep experiencing the universe anew through their eyes[137]. Gull wants to end the story, fix it in time: the Doctor wants to avoid closure, keep going for just one more hour.

---

[136] Tso, Ann, 'English History as Jack the Ripper Tells It: Psychogeography in Alan Moore's *From Hell*'.
[137] 'Meanwhile in the TARDIS', **Doctor Who** Series 5 DVD extra, 2014.

However, there is one thing preventing us from saying that this similarity between the two stories is deliberate: Moore didn't start thinking about writing it until the autumn of 1988[138], shortly before *The Greatest Show* was broadcast. But that isn't to say that **Doctor Who** – and Cartmel specifically – wasn't aware of Alan Moore.

Moore was born in Northampton in 1953[139]. By the 1970s, he was drawing and writing Robert Crumb-esque cartoons for his local newspaper and music magazines while he waited for a career as a punk musician to take off. But with punk stardom remaining elusive and a young family to support – and with drawing taking up too much time – he shifted to concentrate on writing, and in 1980 his association with **Doctor Who** began when he successfully sold some backup strips to Marvel UK's *Doctor Who Weekly*. By 1981, he was a regular contributor to *2000 AD*, and in 1982 was hired as the writer of the series that would bring him to wider attention – **Marvelman**[140].

It was **Doctor Who** that got Moore the gig: the editor who had acquired the rights to **Marvelman** for his new magazine *Warrior* (!982-85) was Dez Skinn, who had bought those first backup strips from Moore. Marvelman was a fairly derivative superhero from 1954, almost a straight copy of Marvel's Captain Marvel and – with his cry of 'Kimota!' to activate his powers – pretty naff. He had been out of print for 20 years, and Skinn was finding it hard to find a writer willing to be associated with him. Most of the modern superheroes that

---

[138] Carpenter, *The British Invasion*, p171. The dates here are a coincidence, as Moore has said frequently that he stopped watching **Doctor Who** at the end of the Hartnell era.
[139] Carpenter, *The British Invasion*, p13.
[140] Carpenter, *The British Invasion*, pp17-18.

were contemporaries of Marvelman had been brought up to date by stripping away the more unbelievable aspects of their characters; remove them from Marvelman, however, and you would have very little left. But – inspired by a satire of Superman from *Mad Magazine* – Moore came up with a strategy that would see him through the rest of his comics career:

> 'It struck me that if you just turn the dial to the same degree in the other direction, by applying real life logic to a superhero, you could make something [...] that was quite startling, sort of dramatic and powerful.'[141]

Moore's **Marvelman** took the character's goofy, derivative backstory and explained it away as an invention of the mad scientist who had really created him, inspired – of course – by comic books. He made Marvelman a half-remembered dream that haunted his alter ego Michael Moran while he went through his life in a decidedly grim and realistic 1980s England. When Moran discovers his powers again, it is an unscrupulous corporate CEO – his grown-up ex-sidekick – who becomes his nemesis. Moore wrote his **Marvelman** for adults, with a satirical eye for the hoary old tropes of the genre but never missing the chance to write real people dealing with real issues in an unexpected and complex way. The resulting comics became classics, putting Moore's name firmly in the minds of the comics industry and fans alike and kicking off revisionist takes on superheroes of all kinds[142].

---

[141] Alan Moore, quoted in Carpenter, *The British Invasion*, p20.
[142] Carpenter, *The British Invasion*, pp18-25.

Moore made postmodernist takes something of a speciality. At the same time as writing **Marvelman**, Moore also wrote *V For Vendetta* (1982-85, 1988-89) for Dez Skinn, his first swipe at Thatcher. He extended her policies into an openly fascist future, and made his hero – V, who started life as another superhero knockoff, this time of Marvel's Nightraven – a moral absolutist who would stop at nothing to bring down the government, and held as much contempt for the public who had allowed them to come to power as he did for those in power themselves[143]. Both comics brought Moore to the attention of Dick Giordano and Karen Berger across the pond at DC Comics, who hired him to revitalise their comic **The Saga of the Swamp Thing** (1982-99), which was on the verge of cancellation. In 1984, Moore took over the reins and – as he had before with **Marvelman** – reworked the character's slightly hokey origins and started writing adult stories of real people facing real problems, but with the added complication of one of them being a lumbering god-vegetable[144].

In 1986, Moore was finally able to finish his **Marvelman** story, which had been interrupted by legal battles that saw the character renamed as Miracleman. But Miracleman's morality had taken a turn towards V's, using his powers to kill those he decides have lost the right to live[145]. That same year, as **Swamp Thing** hit issue #50, Moore combined everything he had learned about writing comics – and all the questions he wanted to ask about the genre – and put them into what some consider his magnum opus: *Watchmen* (1986-87)[146].

---

[143] Carpenter, *The British Invasion*, pp26-28.
[144] Carpenter, *The British Invasion*, pp37-54.
[145] Carpenter, *The British Invasion*, p58.
[146] Carpenter, *The British Invasion*, p61.

As he would later with *From Hell*, Moore put a big clue about the story right in the title, which comes from Juvenal's 'Quis custodiet ipsos custodes?' – 'Who watches the watchmen?' As well as writing compelling, adult drama that uses and subverts the conventions of the medium he was working in, Moore asks his audience to question the very nature of superheroes. The heroes he presents each have their own view of the world, one that is incompatible with any of their peers', and acts within their own moral code to make the world as they would have it. They are characters given free rein to do whatever they want, with no-one able to watch over them, and it leads ultimately to one superhero killing thousands in order to bring about world peace. As he has done throughout his career, Moore used **Watchmen** to try to make his audience engage[147].

> 'We tried to set up four or five radically opposing ways of seeing the world and let the readers figure it out for themselves; let them make a moral decision for once in their miserable lives! Too many writers go for that "baby bird" moralising, where your audience just sits there with their beaks open and you just cram regurgitated morals down their throat. Heroes don't work that way anymore [...] What we wanted to do was show all of these people, warts and all. Show that even the worst of them had something going for them, and even the best of them had their flaws.'[148]

Moore's career continued for many years past 1986, of course, but at the point that Andrew Cartmel was being offered the job of Script

---

[147] Carpenter, *The British Invasion*, pp61-69.
[148] Alan Moore, quoted in Eno, Vincent, and El Csawza, 'Vincent Eno and El Csawza Meet Comics Megastar Alan Moore'.

Editor on **Doctor Who**, these were the things that he knew of it. Certainly, he knew of *Watchmen*, and in particular its blue-skinned hero Dr Manhattan: Manhattan was Moore's take on the atomic superhero type, based on Charlton Comics' Captain Atom character, recently purchased by DC[149]. But in typical Moore style, he truly considered what it would be like to be that kind of person in the real world:

> 'Time, in a post-Einsteinian universe, cannot be regarded in the same way: from what Einstein says, it is possible that the future and past must exist now, for what "now" means. Someone existing in a quantum universe would not see time broken up in the linear way we see it. We tried to think what it would be like to somebody to whom the theory of relativity was what he had for breakfast, more or less [...] if you could see that different aspect of things then it would change you. You would not be able to feel the same way about the importance of human affairs [...] in a lifespan that may span billennia he's only gone a couple of steps. He's growing away from humanity gradually. It's not a cold unemotional thing, it's just different; a different way of seeing the universe.'[150]

For Cartmel, the Doctor was linked to Moore's Doctor Manhattan: both had associations with humans but were not strictly human themselves; both had a relationship to time that looked odd to lesser beings; both were beyond arguments about whether the means justified the ends, by dint of being able to see both the ends and their

---

[149] Carpenter, *The British Invasion*, p61.
[150] Alan Moore, quoted in Eno and El Csawza, 'Comics Megastar Alan Moore'.

own relationship to them long in advance. When Cartmel wrote the audition speech for the new Doctor, it was Doctor Manhattan he was thinking of[151], and he still found the thrust of it relevant when he reworked it for Mel's leaving speech in *Dragonfire*.

Moore – and particularly his **Swamp Thing** comic – 'had been my main inspiration' when Cartmel was offered the job of Script Editor, and in 1987 he made an unsuccessful attempt to get Moore to write for the show. When Stephen Wyatt was starting work on his first **Who** script, *Paradise Towers*, Cartmel gave him a copy of Moore's **The Ballad of Halo Jones** (1984) which influenced the Kangs in that story, and it was one of Moore's **Swamp Thing** stories that inspired the Haemovores in Ian Briggs' *The Curse of Fenric* (1989)[152]. Ironically, **Doctor Who** itself also had a small part to play in the end of Moore's comics career: it was an argument over Marvel UK republishing Moore's **Doctor Who** backup strips in the USA without any royalty payments that led Moore to cut all ties with the company[153], and meant that when a similar falling out occurred with DC he had very few places left within comics where he could work.

But if Moore was the 'main inspiration' for Cartmel when he started on **Doctor Who**, can we trace how this expressed itself? The direct references we can see are tangential at best, so what was it Cartmel was inspired to do by **Swamp Thing** and its author?

To me, it seems that Moore's fingerprints are all over the Cartmel era, because he set the pattern that Cartmel decided to follow for

---

[151] Cartmel, *Script Doctor*, p25.
[152] Stephen Wyatt, author's own interview; Cartmel, *Script Doctor*, pp184-87.
[153] Carpenter, *The British Invasion*, p54.

reinvigorating the show. When Cartmel was invited to become **Doctor Who**'s Script Editor, he found himself in the same position that Moore had been when asked to write **Swamp Thing**: take something that nobody really cared about any more, something that was too silly and divorced from reality to be anything but a joke to the established audience and make it work anyway. Do something that nobody really expected could be done, and in doing it kickstart a career that would last for a lifetime.

The most obvious link is in making the Doctor more like Dr Manhattan: not just in his unique relationship to the Einsteinian 'now' but also in his sense of a morality that isn't quite human any more. Under Cartmel, the Doctor destroys Skaro and a Cyberman fleet, he manipulates Ace for reasons that never quite become clear and starts treating other people like pawns that can be moved around the board to suit his ends. He puts in place the 'One warning: that's all you get' approach that has become the norm for most of his later incarnations. And, of course, Cartmel starts to tentatively rewrite the Doctor's origin story in a very Moore-ish fashion: not by completely overwriting it, but by introducing new ideas that suggest that what we thought we knew might be true from a certain point of view, but that point of view didn't take in the full picture. Cartmel's Doctor can be read as Cartmel's idea of what Moore would have done with him, as is most easily seen in stories like *The Happiness Patrol* (1988), essentially a Cartmelian take on *V for Vendetta*.

On top of that, like Moore, Cartmel tries to bring a sense of the real world back to **Doctor Who**, to engage with real-life issues: *Remembrance of the Daleks* digs into real racism; *The Happiness Patrol* the power and necessity of sadness and grief; *The Greatest Show* the 80s abandonment of 60s idealism; *Silver Nemesis*... well, every rule needs an exception, but there is at least an effort to engage with the Cybermen as a symbol of Nazi ideals of the ubermensch that echoes Moore's treatment of superheroes. This is the period in the show's history where Cartmel tries to bring the TARDIS back to the real world, in part because he knew the BBC design department could cope with that better, but also because that was part of Moore's revisionist blueprint. And that is what did for quarries during the Cartmel era:

> 'One of my preoccupations on **Doctor Who** [...] was to [...] try and achieve authentically sinister alien settings. [...] Quarries were the bane of **Doctor Who**.'[154]

Cartmel wanted to bring the real world back to **Doctor Who**, and if he was going to convince anyone that **Doctor Who** was different now, quarries would have to go, except in the case of stories where there was a genuine need to show a desolate world[155]. That was what Moore would have done in Cartmel's position, and it's hard to argue that Cartmel was wrong, because his era is now generally seen as the point at which **Doctor Who** picked itself up, dusted itself down and got on with being good again. It put in place so many of the little tricks and tropes that the modern series adopted that it is possible to see Russell T Davies' first series as a continuation of the 26 years that went before it. Cartmel made the right decisions at the right time, and brought **Doctor Who** back from the brink just enough to

---

[154] Cartmel, *Script Doctor*, pp135-40.
[155] The show had been satirising itself regarding quarries since *Destiny of the Daleks* in 1979, after all.

give it a chance of a future. And the most important lesson he learned from Moore was that first of all, the stories had to be good.

But that doesn't mean that Cartmel gave us the **Doctor Who** that Moore would have made.

Grant Morrison despaired at the popularity of *Watchmen*, in part because it spawned the idea that comics had to be grim and dark to be good, whereas he liked the fact that comics could be strange, and bright, and garish and fun[156]. In **Doctor Who** terms, it's the argument that **Doctor Who** is only really **Doctor Who** when Philip Hinchcliffe is making it, and Graham Williams was an aberration. Moore's work was thoughtful and transformative, with a lot of subtleties that were easy to miss: the darkness and moral ambiguity were easier to see, and many writers emulated them because they were exciting and new, even if they didn't always fit the story. And to a certain degree, Cartmel did too[157].

The thing that Moore did more than anything else was to use the tools of comics to get the effect he wanted, all the time using that effect to comment on the medium itself. He was truly postmodern in his approach, writing always on two levels, commentary and meta-commentary. He used the juxtaposition between two panels on the page or the art and its accompanying text to create a tension or an irony that forced his readers to engage more deeply with what was on the page[158]. He had characters discuss ideas – the ridiculousness

---

[156] Carpenter, *The British Invasion*, p119.

[157] This is not to denigrate Cartmel or his abilities as a script editor and writer: the sub-category of writers labelled 'Not as good as Alan Moore' is rather large, and definitely includes myself.

[158] Carpenter, *The British Invasion*, p31.

of costumed heroes, or the importance of uniformity and house style – that, whilst rooted in his story, could also be seen as comments on his industry[159]. He created multiple conflicting moralities within *Watchmen*, not to say that all superheroes should be morally ambiguous but to encourage his readers to question the moral implications of the superhero genre as a whole[160].

It is rare in Cartmel's **Doctor Who** to find other moral viewpoints that are as centred, coherent and convincing as the Doctor's: Morgaine[161] would be a prominent example of a character who clearly operates to a relatable moral code that is in opposition to the Doctor's, but by the end of the story she has still accepted that she is wrong and the Doctor is right. Certainly, in *The Greatest Show* and the other stories around it, nothing encourages the audience to question too hard what the Doctor does, and the antagonists aren't presented as having an opposing moral position they are motivated by that the audience might agree with. The Doctor is morally ambiguous, but not to make a comment on his elevated status as the hero of his own TV show and how it allows him to inflict his morality on his universe. He does things that are sometimes morally questionable, and most of the time we don't really notice, because he is the hero of his own TV show and so is probably right. Cartmel was quoted in 1994 saying 'We certainly did want to build up the mystery. Having said that, we had no agenda'[162]; the darkness, the mystery, were the intended

---

[159] Carpenter, *The British Invasion*, p34.

[160] Carpenter, *The British Invasion*, p68.

[161] *Battlefield*.

[162] Cartmel in Howe, David J, Mark Stammers and Steven J Walker, *The Handbook: The Unofficial and Unauthorised Guide to the Production of Doctor Who* Volume 2, loc 11749.

result, not a tool to push the audience to start their own interrogation of the text.

There is very little commentary on television or **Doctor Who** in Cartmel's era, and also relatively little use of the conventions and tropes of television to highlight those tropes: nothing of the ilk of Martin Jarvis' Governor directing a cliffhanger crash zoom in *Vengeance on Varos* (1985)[163]. Cartmel has learned some of the techniques Moore was using – most notably the trick of writing something good to attract an audience – but he doesn't use them to the same ends that Moore uses them. And it works for him, in part because Cartmel is right that **Doctor Who** is the kind of show where those techniques can work: when he moves to **Casualty** (1986-), he is less successful, and in part that is because it is harder to apply the formula that worked in **Doctor Who** to **Casualty**. Whereas it is possible to see how Moore's approach to outdated comic book superheroes – an interrogation of the morals and conventions of the genre – could work for either show.

And that is why I'd argue that *The Greatest Show* is the best place to see what Andrew Cartmel would have liked his **Doctor Who** to be, because it is the story that most closely matches the idea of what Moore's techniques could have done with TV **Doctor Who**. It has the superficial elements – the darker, more mysterious and morally ambiguous Doctor starting to take shape – but also some of the postmodernist intent: the juxtaposition of clowns and hearses to provoke engagement from the viewer; the meta-text investigating the problems of the previous era and demonstrating the present's ability to overcome them. It represents possibly the pinnacle of what

---

[163] Sandifer, *TARDIS Eruditorum 6*, p488.

a postmodern approach to **Doctor Who** could produce, and the depth of potential for the show to be interesting, relevant and above all entertaining, that caused it to survive the 1990s.

FINGERPRINTS OF THE GODS

The debate about whether **Doctor Who** is science fiction or fantasy has been going for a long time, and both sides can claim members of different production teams over the years. Orson Scott Card apparently said 'science fiction has rivets and fantasy has trees', but that doesn't help much when your space station has rivets but is populated by sentient trees[164]. We might have more success with Lynda Carter's explanation ('Sci-fi is when Wonder Woman fights villains from outer space, fantasy is thinking Wonder Woman will go on a date with you'[165]) if we substitute the Doctor for Wonder Woman. Andrew Cartmel, however, was very much on the side of science fiction: he praised his favourite writers and stories by their relationship to the genre[166], and his main objection to Pip and Jane Baker as writers was that 'their take on science fiction in general and **Doctor Who** in particular was old fashioned.'[167] Which makes the fact that Cartmel's era of the show so consistently presented us with magic without couching it in pseudo-science so surprising.

In the past, if the Doctor had been fighting the Devil in a church in middle England, then he was first sure to pronounce 'Everything that happens in life must have a scientific explanation. If you know where

---

[164] *The End of the World* (2005).

[165] Carter, Lynda, Tweet posted 27 September 2022.

[166] Praising Ben Aaronovitch, for example, in Cartmel*, Script Doctor*, p17, or the stories he commissioned for Season 24 in Cartmel*, Script Doctor*, p97.

[167] Cartmel, *Script Doctor*, p31. John Nathan-Turner, conversely, seemed to see the show as Light Entertainment of the old school kind, and so his fondness for 'the Baker twins' can be understood in that light.

to look for it, that is,'[168], and it was a general rule that you could tell how sympathetic we were meant to be towards any particular 'primitive species' by how superstitious they were[169]. But in *The Greatest Show*, we are presented with werewolves, zombies and ancient gods without so much of a whiff of scientific fig-leaf[170]. For someone so convinced that he was making science fiction, Cartmel certainly didn't mind getting a little fantasy on him.

Perhaps this is just another symptom of Cartmel following Alan Moore's revisionism: Moore has been a 'practising magician' since making a drunken declaration on his 40th birthday[171], and even before that his work tended towards the more magical. Part of his revision of Swamp Thing's origin story, for example, removed the scientific explanation for the lead character's powers and made him instead a mystical creature, and his DC comics usually involved more of the company's magical beings than their superpowered ones. However, this does create a tension, a feeling that something is amiss.

In later tie-in stories, the Gods are tied into a wider idea as beings from the time before time, the Great Old Ones[172]. This origin linked a number of different adversaries, including Fenric, the Toymaker

---

[168] *The Daemons*, Episode One.

[169] Orthia, Lindy, 'Enlightenment Was the Choice: **Doctor Who** and the Democratisation of Science'.

[170] Yes, Mags is described as 'rather an unusual little specimen' from the planet Vulpana, but no attempt is made to suggest that the planet is inhabited by werewolf-like aliens, or that Mags doesn't just happen to be an alien who has also been struck down by lycanthropy.

[171] Leith, Sam. '*Watchmen* Author Alan Moore: "I'm Definitely Done with Comics"'.

[172] Lane, Andy, *All-Consuming Fire*, pp216-17.

and the Great Intelligence – mostly god-like beings who had had little or no on-screen science fiction rationale given to them previously. This does suggest a certain tension around these characters: that they needed to be tidied up and explained, grouped together and given something that could pass as a scientific explanation, if only by **Doctor Who**'s slightly dubious standards. When writing his own tie-in novels, however[173], Cartmel didn't take the opportunity to resolve this tension. He even went so far as to undermine the science fiction explanations other stories had given us for staples of the show like the Doctor or the TARDIS:

> 'You don't believe in magic but you believe in machines. So when he explained himself to you, he used your terms of reference. That's the way a sorcerer behaves. [...] Let me tell you something about yourself [...] When you were a kid your favourite reading was science fiction. Maybe books, maybe comics. Space ships, time travel, that sort of thing. [...] You don't believe in magic but you believe he's from another planet and you're his girl companion [...] And that thing in the cellar. The door. The gateway to other worlds. How does he account for that? A space ship? A time machine?'[174]

In the book from which this speech comes, this bothers Ace so much that she physically attacks the speaking character, Justine, presumably because she has forgotten meeting a unicorn in the previous novel[175]. In fact, the Doctor had only recently told Ace that

---

[173] As part of the Virgin **New Adventures** book series.

[174] Justine's side of dialogue from Cartmel, Andrew, *Cat's Cradle: Warhead*, pp163-64.

[175] Hunt, Andrew, *Cat's Cradle: Witch Mark*.

magic was real, if you read the Target novelisations – as the New Adventures target audience most definitely had:

'How does it fly then?'

'Magic!'

'Oh, what? Be feasible, Doctor.'

'I thought I was a Professor. What's Clarke's Law?'

[...]

'Any sufficiently advanced technology is indistinguishable from magic.'

'Well, the reverse is also true.'[176]

However, Justine's description of Ace as a childhood science fiction fan doesn't quite ring true of what we know of her either: lighting fires on Horsenden Hill or hanging out with her mates at the youth club, getting warnings from the police[177], making her own gelignite and blowing up class 1C's prize winning pottery pig collection[178], and then nipping home to bury her nose in **The Ballad of Halo Jones**? No, Justine's description sounds more like she is talking about Cartmel himself, or more likely the kind of people that Cartmel might have imagined would be reading the seventh book in a new line of **Doctor Who** novels: it seems that Cartmel is attempting to talk directly to the reader, to ask them to question what the TV stories have always told them about the Doctor's origins. He primes us – as he did

---

[176] Platt, Marc, *Battlefield*, p88. This was based on a scene cut from transmission later included in the 2008 DVD special edition.
[177] *Survival*, Part One.
[178] *Battlefield*, Part One.

75

occasionally during his time as Script Editor – to think that a Moore-ish revision of the Doctor's hokey old backstory is on its way. But was it magic specifically that Cartmel thought **Doctor Who** needed more of?

Fan lore suggests that Cartmel had a very definite goal for the series: the Cartmel Masterplan. Awareness of the plan grew out of fan speculation on where a number of hints dropped through seasons 25 and 26 might be going, but first became definite when 'Gallifrey – Notes on the Planet's Background' was published as an appendix in Lance Parkin's *A History of the Universe* (1996). This was billed as 'virtually the whole text of a document [...] (from ideas prepared for the **Doctor Who** TV series) by Andrew Cartmel, Ben Aaronovitch and Marc Platt'[179]. Parkin's appendix details the ancient history of Gallifrey, but omits the section on the Doctor's role in it – namely that he is a technological reincarnation of a contemporary of Rassilon and Omega known only as the Other – as this was to form the climax of Platt's upcoming novel *Lungbarrow* (1997). Paul Cornell then built on this to introduce the idea that the Seventh Doctor was Time's Champion[180], the agent of an Eternal named Time worshipped as a god by the Time Lords, using whatever means he could to ensure history progressed as it should.

In some ways, the reason for all this was sex.

The way it was explained in the **New Adventures**, Time Lord society was asexual and only reproduced by growing new Gallifreyans on 'looms' from raw genetic material. In the early 90s, this was a

---

[179] Parkin, Lance. *A History of the Universe,* pp269-73.
[180] Bishop, David, 'A Conversation with Paul Cornell'.

concern for a number of **Doctor Who** fans who had taken JNT's 'no hanky-panky in the TARDIS'[181] rule as law and were keen to argue that the Doctor did not have sex. These fans managed to construct a 'problem of Susan' by ignoring the textual explanation for why Susan calls the Doctor 'grandfather' – that she **is** his granddaughter - and performed extreme contortions to make it fit with the entirely fan-constructed idea that the Doctor was asexual, even going so far as to suggest that 'grandfather' is actually a term of endearment that doesn't imply a familial relationship[182]. Virgin's 'official' answer to why a granddaughter calls her grandfather grandfather was that Susan was the Other's granddaughter, but thought the Doctor was close enough[183].

This may seem strange in the era following *The Doctor Dances* (2005), but as a fan who came of age at the end of the 80s and moved online in the early 90s, I can understand this conflicted relationship with sex. This was the era of AIDS, and in particular the 1987 UK Government's 'Monolith' public service advertisement, in which the man who would later play the War Doctor announced:

> 'There is now a danger that has become a threat to us all. It is a deadly disease and there is no known cure...'[184]

---

[181] 'John Nathan-Turner,' *The Times*.

[182] Some fans still cling to this redefinition of language: for instance, the online user Rooks who claimed in a forum post that 'Only the new series has made reference to a child, the old series contained no references to family.' (Rooks, comment on the *Digital Spy Forum*.)

[183] Platt, Marc, *Lungbarrow*, pp195-97.

[184] McCallum, Simon, 'Beyond the Tombstone: How British TV Responded to the AIDS Crisis'.

On top of the usual adolescent fears about sex, the advert effectively told a generation of teens that having sex could kill them; with the introduction of Section 28 in 1988[185] – legislation introduced by the Government that forbade the 'promotion' of homosexuality in education, and which was widely complied with by avoiding any mention of it whatsoever – it meant that proper discussion of AIDS and the relative risks of catching it was much harder to have. It's not surprising that 90s fandom had a strange attitude to sex, veering between insisting that the Doctor would never have had it – and definitely not with any of his companions – and obsessing over who Ace had and hadn't had sex with[186].

And perhaps Cartmel was the same. Perhaps his plan for his tenure as Script Editor definitely included confirmation that the Doctor hadn't had sex but had hung out with Rassilon and Omega, and it was only the end of **Doctor Who** as a TV series that stopped us seeing it. Certainly, many fans have taken it to mean just that[187]. However, this is a slightly problematic interpretation for a number of reasons.

Firstly, Parkin tells us that the Notes document was written on 9 November 1990 at the request of Virgin Publishing[188], nearly a year

---

[185] More formally, Section 28 of the Local Government Act 1988. See McCallum, 'Beyond the Tombstone' for details of British TV's reaction to Clause 28.

[186] Ace was possibly the only 20th century given any kind of overt sexuality, but the Virgin **New Adventures** in particular seemed to be obsessed with the subject at times.

[187] TheObsessedWhovian95, 'Doctor Who Retrospective 10: The Cartmel Master Plan' or Sao Til, 'What was the Cartmel Masterplan? | Doctor Who'.

[188] Parkin, *A History of the Universe*, p269.

after *Survival* aired and at a point at which it was clear that Season 27 would not be happening any time soon. The document was written as background for Virgin's **New Adventures** series, which was billed as the direct continuation of **Doctor Who** after the TV series ended: clearly Virgin had a vested interest in linking the Cartmel Masterplan directly to his time as Script Editor and implying it was what he would have done on TV if he'd had the chance. Another issue is that the Masterplan itself only directly impacted the plot of two books in the **New Adventures**, *Cat's Cradle: Time's Crucible* (1992) and the aforementioned *Lungbarrow*, both by Marc Platt and both based on stories pitched for the TV series and rejected by Cartmel[189]. Certainly it wasn't a point of discussion during the making of *The Greatest Show*, which was the very next story produced after the story that includes the first televised link between the Doctor and ancient Gallifrey[190]. as Wyatt explained in 2023:

> 'I was never really any part of discussions of the "Masterplan". Indeed, Ace's line in [episode] 4, "It was your show all along, wasn't it?" is the only time I got near it.'[191]

Another thing to note would be that the teams behind both **Doctor Who** on television and the **New Adventures** book series were clearly making it up as they went along. The Other, for example, had first

---

[189] Cartmel does say it was Producer John Nathan-Turner who stopped work on 'Lungbarrow', but agrees it was the right decision as the ideas weren't coalescing into an actual story. Cartmel, *Script Doctor*, pp194-97.

[190] The Doctor's ambiguous 'And didn't we have trouble with the prototype,' when talking about the Hand of Omega in *Remembrance of the Daleks*.

[191] Stephen Wyatt, author's own interview.

been named in Ben Aaronovitch's novelisation of *Remembrance of the Daleks* (1990), which predated the Virgin notes by a number of months. In it, he is referred to without capitalisation – indicating that he is just the other person in the room – and destined to 'vanish altogether from history' [192]. By the time he is mentioned in *Lungbarrow* (1997), however, he has become 'the Other'[193] and has the holiday of Otherstide celebrated annually in his honour[194]. In the initial discussions, Cartmel states that the Other is straightforwardly the Doctor[195], whereas by *Lungbarrow* his origin is tied into various ongoing plot threads so that the Other was a different person, but one who shared enough essence with the Doctor to be recognisable to close family[196]. Even in *The Greatest Show*, there is evidence that Cartmel's thinking was still developing: the story starts with the Doctor only being made aware of the Psychic Circus by the junkmail that invades his TARDIS, leading to him seeming to take Ace there on a whim, but by the end of the story, history has rewritten itself and the whole adventure has become part of a plan by the Doctor to face and defeat the Gods[197].

But the biggest issue with the idea of the Cartmel Masterplan revealing what Cartmel was definitely going to do in his next season of **Doctor Who** is that it goes against the plan that Cartmel has always stated he did have.

---

[192] Aaronovitch, Ben, *Remembrance of the Daleks,* p46.

[193] Platt, *Lungbarrow*, p136.

[194] Platt, *Lungbarrow*, p40.

[195] Cartmel, *Script Doctor,* p156.

[196] Platt, *Lungbarrow*, pp195-197.

[197] Cartmel*, Script Doctor*, pp141-142.

'Andrew and I both thought the show had got very self-absorbed and in some ways was disappearing up its own bottom.'[198]

The last season before Cartmel took over typifies the problem he saw: a whole season devoted to the fictionalisation of **Doctor Who**'s behind the scenes problems, played out with Time Lords in silly costumes, taking the place of real drama. The two big revelations from the season – that the Time Lords moved the Earth, and that the Valeyard is some kind of future incarnation of the Doctor – both mean little to the casual viewer and reenforce the Doctor's passivity in relation to the other Time Lords who are proactively putting their plans into action. Whilst it is clear that discussion of the history of Gallifrey and the Doctor being the Other did happen prior to *Ghost Light* being commissioned, it is equally clear that it was put to one side as inappropriate for season 26 and only later revisited when Virgin heard about it[199]. It can just as easily be argued that the hints about his background that the seventh Doctor drops indicate he knows he is the Timeless Child who gave Gallifrey regeneration[200], and just as unlikely that this was what Cartmel was going to reveal in a 1990 season.

Cartmel's justification for the work he was doing with Aaronovitch and Platt on the Doctor's backstory was explained (again, many years after the fact) as being because:

'I was tired of the notion of the Doctor as a mere Time Lord

---

[198] Wyatt in Griffiths, 'Oh What a Circus.'
[199] Platt, 'Introduction' to *Lungbarrow*.
[200] *The Timeless Children* (2020).

amongst other Time Lords. He had started off in 1963 in the shape of William Hartnell as a scary enigma, a being of unlimited mystery. He could have remained a total enigma. [...] Explanations had ruined the Doctor. The trajectory of his mysterious character had been one of steady decline. First we had no idea who or what he was. Then we learned he was a Time Lord. Then we learned he was a Time Lord among other Time Lords. And, the next thing you know, he was the kind of chump who could be put on trial by the other Time Lords, and generally be pushed around with impunity. So I set about restoring the awe, mystery and strength to the character.'[201]

Cartmel had great success with the first stage of the plan – reintroducing 'the awe, mystery and strength' but the proposed second stage – confirming that the Doctor had been a contemporary of Rassilon and Omega – hadn't begun, and indeed had already been abandoned for Season 26 as soon as any real thought was put into how it might actually work. By the end of 1989 it was clear that **Doctor Who** wasn't coming back, and a monologue had to be inserted at the end of *Survival* to provide some kind of closure for the series. Some work had been done on a theoretical Season 27, but nothing was developed beyond a few one-line ideas: as soon as Cartmel stopped being paid to think about **Doctor Who** and started getting paid to think about **Casualty**, all work on those ideas would have stopped.

Whilst it is possible that the vague story idea of Ace leaving the Doctor to enrol in the Academy on Gallifrey might have developed into something that also told us the Doctor and the Other were the

---

[201] Cartmel, *Script Doctor*, p155.

same person, it's equally possible that it wouldn't. Because – as Cartmel had already expressed – if you want something to be mysterious, the last thing you should do is spend any time telling its origin story. Having the Doctor drop hints that he might have been around when the Hand of Omega was tested is an enigma; having him categorically shown to be the Other is just another explanation.

With hindsight, Cartmel may enjoy the narrative that his era was building towards a climax that was denied us, but none of his decisions, statements or actions at the time show any sign of **Doctor Who** heading in the direction of more answers. Even in 1992, with the meta-narrative of the lost Cartmel Masterplan being written by Virgin, and given the opportunity of telling the story he'd apparently wanted to for three years, Cartmel shied away from giving any explanations. Yes, Justine says that the Doctor is a magician and we've been wrong all these years, but Cartmel doesn't set her up as a character that we should listen to, nor even like. She is an over-emotional teenager, sure that she knows everything and set in opposition to Ace, one of the more successful TV companions: if Cartmel had wanted us to believe the Doctor might be a magician, it would have been Ace who made the speech, not Justine.

What the argument sets up – quite successfully – is a little seed of doubt; not that Justine is definitely right, but that she could be. Her explanation of the Doctor as a magician with a gateway to other worlds isn't right, but it isn't self-evidently wrong: that is why Ace resorts to violence, because Justine is right that a magician who said he was an alien with a time machine wouldn't look any different to the Doctor. Cartmel asks us to think about the things we've always believed about the Doctor – that he is a Time Lord, that he ran away from Gallifrey out of boredom, that he is just a madman with a box

– and wonder if maybe there isn't a different explanation of the same facts that we aren't seeing because our assumptions blind us. If I was too harsh on Cartmel in the previous chapter for not applying Moore's revisionist method with enough consideration to what he was actually doing, then I should give him full credit for this adaptation: the Doctor didn't need an updated, more realistic origin story and Cartmel knew it – what he needed was a little more ambiguity.

And that was the way that Cartmel used magic across his era; his refusal to give an explanation – as the show always had before – leaves space for mystery, Yes, the Gods of Ragnarok **might** be aliens with godlike powers, or they might be magical beings. The important thing isn't what the explanation is, it's the enigma. It pulls you into the story, asks you to come up with your own answers, to let the story live in your head even after the credits roll. An explanation pushes you out, lets you file it away and move on to something else. *The Greatest Show* is the first time Cartmel and the writers he commissioned had the chance to put that into practice, and so it is the first time that we get to see a little unexplained magic in the show.

But that isn't to say that there isn't more to it than just that.

At first glance, Mags the werewolf seems to be just another example of Cartmel's twin urges to destabilise the audience's prior knowledge of the Doctor with unexplained magic, and to get as many cool young girls into the show as he could. Indeed, Stephen Wyatt didn't think there was more behind her creation than just 'We thought werewolves were a strong image'[202], and a need to give his pseudo-

---

[202] Wyatt in Griffiths, 'Honk, the Squonk and a Green Non-Entity'.

Doctor character a pseudo-companion. But in a story where the main antagonists are named as 'the Gods of Ragnarok' it does evoke one of Cartmel's other themes: Norse mythology.

The most famous reference point for this is *The Curse of Fenric*, where again we have an antagonist named for Viking legend. Fenric, the evil genie trapped in a bottle, is also Fenrir, leader of wolves and chained due to trickery, ready to throw off his chains and play his part in the end of the world. Ian Briggs deliberately used Fenrir as an inspiration for Fenric, and left signposts in the various references to wolves (the story was called 'Wolftime' and 'The Wolves of Fenric' before the final title was settled on), the importance of Vikings to the story and Commander Millington's obsession with Norse mythology[203].

The original Fenrir is an interesting character, at once a dangerous demi-god destined to devour Odin but also a tragic figure, only becoming a monster in response to the Æsir's mistrust and his best friend Tyr's betrayal of him. He demonstrates the Vikings' ambivalent attitude towards wolves, admiring their strength and pack mentality but – as a mainly agricultural society – fearing their impact on livestock. Odin is destined to be devoured by a wolf, but happily keeps two wolves by his side at all times as companions. And this ambivalence is demonstrated by other stories the Vikings told themselves, stories about werewolves[204].

---

[203] Sullivan, Shannon Patrick, *'The Curse of Fenric'*.
[204] Durn, Sarah, 'The Long, Hidden History of the Viking Obsession With Werewolves'.

One of the oldest werewolf stories in the world comes from the Vikings, the story of Sigmundr and Sinfjötli, telling how father and son thieves discovered wolfskins that transformed them into savage wolves when they put them on. It is one of over 50 different stories of werewolves that the Vikings would tell each other for entertainment, the earliest being connected to war and unchained savagery, whilst the later tales tend towards the 'romantic werewolf' who is a tragic victim of their curse[205]. In some ways, Fenrir is the grandfather of them all, containing both the savagery and the sympathy of the other tales; what else is a werewolf but a savage beast chained within a human skin? And what else is Mags but Fenrir, betrayed by her apparent friend and eventually freed to revenge herself? By including Mags – whether he knew it or not – Wyatt was tapping into this history, forging another link with the story already referenced by the Gods of Ragnarok.

Ragnarok – Ragnarøkkr in the 13th Century Eddas the story was eventually recorded in – is the story of the end of the Norse world, where the land would be destroyed by the seas and the ancient evils would be free again, including Fenrir and Jörmungandr – also known as the Great Serpent and again referenced in *The Curse of Fenric*. It tells how the Æsir were destined to die: Ragnarøkkr is usually translated as 'the Twilight of the Gods', which gave Wagner his title for his opera *Götterdämmerung* (1876) and us – via Nazi admiration for it – a tenuous link back to *Silver Nemesis* and De Flores' Neo-Nazi paramilitaries. The Vikings always knew that their gods were destined to die, and interestingly their gods did too: Odin gave his eye for knowledge, which included the knowledge of the tale of

---

[205] Durn, 'The Long, Hidden History'.

Ragnarok. The Æsir lived their lives in full knowledge that the end was coming, doing whatever they could – like the chaining of Fenrir – to delay it but never able to completely avert it. In many ways, this makes it the perfect mythology for late-80s **Doctor Who** to start referencing: it too knew that everything it did was just delaying the inevitable. The end was definitely coming.

The Greatest Show also includes in its last episode another brief reference to a different kind of magic that suggests an alternative interpretation. As the Doctor waits for his friends to bring the eye medallion to him in the Gods' arena, he attempts to entertain his adversaries. The magic that the Doctor deploys is fairly dated – more akin to the music hall than the work of Paul Daniels or David Copperfield, which were popular at the time[206] – and it is possible we are intended to see this as more metaphorical evidence that **Doctor Who** is old-fashioned and unable to satisfy the unreasonable demands of BBC management or its audience. But for a few brief moments, the Doctor performs an escapology act, suspended (apparently from nothing) upside-down as he tries to escape from a straitjacket. In the moment we see, he kicks one leg behind the other, struggling against his bonds, and he for a moment resembles something else from the world of magic: the Hanged Man.

The Hanged Man is a card from the Major Arcana of Tarot, and in some decks is depicted as Odin hanging upside-down from the Tree of Knowledge to gain his presentiment of Ragnarok, which does tie in neatly with **Doctor Who**'s other Norse references[207]. Because of this, one of the interpretations of the card if it occurs during a

---

[206] Adam and Erik, '*The Greatest Show in the Galaxy*'.
[207] Butler, Bill, *The Definitive Tarot*, p153.

reading is that of knowledge gained through self-sacrifice, of current difficulties making you better equipped to face the future: one of the words associated with the card is 'regeneration'[208]. If the show had been getting its cards read and the Hanged Man had appeared, the reader would have divined that it was going through a difficult time but that it would return bigger and stronger in the future because of it. Perhaps I'm reading too much into this brief moment of screen time – except that the card is foreshadowed earlier, as Morgana draws it from the pack whilst doing a reading for the Doctor in episode two: it would seem she takes the idea of seeing his future very literally. It is also backed up by the medallion that the Doctor is waiting for when he ends up in this pose: the eye design resembles the Eye of Horus, which – as well as representing well-being and healing – is also a symbol of regeneration. Horus supposedly had his eye torn out by Set only to have it regrown or otherwise returned, and when it was given to the dead god Osiris it gave them the power to sustain themselves into the afterlife[209].

So, we have two symbols of current adversity leading to future success in the same few seconds of screen time, linked back to the story of Ragnarok, where even the head of the pantheon Odin is destined to die. Probably they weren't deliberate[210], but that doesn't

---

[208] Reed, Gary, *Book of Tarot*, p10.

[209] Pinch, Geraldine, *Egyptian Mythology*, p132. The same stories also mention the similar destruction and regrowth of Set's testicles, meaning the medallion could have had a very different design indeed.

[210] 'I'm afraid I chose the name because it sounded good. Which was tough on Ian Briggs who I think could have used the name more relevantly in *Curse of Fenric*.' (Stephen Wyatt, author's own interview).

stop them being apposite, because that isn't the whole story of Ragnarok: what happens after the death and the floods and destruction is that the world is left cleansed and fertile. The sun's daughter takes her place in the heavens and the surviving children of the Æsir emerge to watch over the two surviving humans Líf and Lífþrasir as they repopulate the world[211]. The story of Ragnarok is also one of regeneration, and ultimately hope. It tells us that although the future looks bleak, and the things we love are going to die, they will come back stronger than ever. In this world where magic is a possibility, **Doctor Who** is suddenly introducing some very powerful symbols.

For Alan Moore, the act of creativity and magic are inextricably linked:

> 'I believe exactly that art and magic – specifically writing, but art in general, and magic – are almost completely interchangeable. They share the same terminology, they match up in nearly every respect [...] The first magical act was the act of representation – just saying "this means that".'[212]

This sounds like a kind of sympathetic magic, whereby the act of saying 'this means that' gives you power over both this and that. *The Greatest Show* does have an act of sympathetic magic in it: it gives us the ritual sacrifice of a symbol of the show's fans, the people who saw it as not as good as its glory days and useful only for arguing points of trivia over. Then it creates an allegory of precisely where **Doctor Who** was at the time it was made, highlighting every obstacle, every distraction from being the best show it could possibly be. And

---

[211] Garrison, Tom, *Norse Mythology*, p79.
[212] Martin, Tim, 'Everything and Moore', *Aeon*, 17 October 2014.

then it shows them all as surmountable, all things that could be defeated by this new Doctor and this new companion – by this new **team** – and declares right at the end that this is and always was the Doctor's show after all. And if this is sympathetic magic, then its intended result is obvious: in defeating the obstacles within the fiction, they would also be defeated in real life. But Moore's particular brand of magic isn't about practical results, or – more accurately – all magic and creativity brings the same practical result:

> 'They were enabling the creator to pass information on to other conscious minds, even to those existing in the future long after the perpetrator was dead.'[213]

Perhaps the production team were pre-emptively following Moore once more. Maybe their act of magic was simply to creatively document all the barriers in front of them, fixing them in time for the **Doctor Who** of the future to see, and hopefully avoid.

---

[213] Ó Méalóid, Pádraig. 'Alan Moore's Secret Q&A Cult Exposed! Part IV: At Last the Truth Can Be Told!!!!!'

FORWARD

When Ricco Ross' Ringmaster enters the ring to deliver his welcome to the audience, it represents one of the few times that hip hop crosses over with **Doctor Who**. It is the first time any rap is heard on the show, and the last until The Streets' 'Don't Mug Yourself' is anachronistically heard playing from Pete Tyler's car in *Father's Day* (2005). Before we get too excited about **Doctor Who** being an early adopter of this new genre, though, it's worth remembering that while 1988 was the year that hip hop truly broke out in the UK[214], its generally agreed birthday occurred between *The Green Death* (1973) and *The Time Warrior* (1973).

Hip hop's roots are in the dub scene and the sound systems that grew popular in Jamaica after the Second World War and subsequent emigration had depleted the island of musicians; the less labour intensive alternative of a music selector with a powerful amplifier and a bank of homemade speakers became so popular that by the 1960s live bands were largely obsolete[215]. But hip hop was born in the Bronx, New York, an area that had suffered over a decade of presidentially-approved 'benign neglect': those who could afford to move away (mostly white residents) fled, and those that couldn't were forced to endure wages of half the New York City average and a housing system so broken that the best way of making money out of property was to burn it down for the insurance. Between 1973 and 1977, 30,000 fires were set in the South Bronx following the city

---

[214] Emery, Andrew, *Wiggaz with Attitude*, p81.
[215] Procter, Ryan, 'Old To The New Q&A – MC Mell'O' (Part One)'; Chang, Jeff, *Can't Stop, Won't Stop: A History of the Hip-Hop Generation*, pp29, 34-36.

politicians' removal of seven fire companies[216]. Gangs filled the vacuum left by governmental neglect, and after the 1971 murder of local gang member Black Benjie while he was trying to stop a fight, it looked like the city would explode into all out war[217].

Instead – without the support of the police or the local government – the unthinkable happened: the gangs brokered a truce in honour of their fallen comrade. The Bronx wasn't transformed overnight, and it didn't become a paradise, but the delicate truce held long enough for block parties – the transplanted cousins of the Jamaican sound systems – to happen, at first as an attempt to bring the different gangs together socially, but eventually becoming just the thing to do at the weekend[218]. In August 1973, a DJ called Kool Herc performed at his sister's 'Back to School Jam' block party, the first step in a career that saw him become the undisputed champion of the local DJ scene. As his career progressed, he developed his 'merry-go-round' technique of using two copies of the same record, two turntables and two amplifiers to isolate sections of records and loop them to give the dancers he christened B-Boys and B-Girls more time to do their thing[219].

One of the people to connect with what DJ Kool Herc was doing was the young gang 'warlord' and DJ who would become Afrika Bambaataa. As his popularity as a DJ grew, drawing in crowds made up of several rival gangs, Bambaataa saw in the block parties and various subcultures that had coalesced around them – the B-Boy and

---

[216] Chang, *Can't Stop, Won't Stop*, pp13-15.
[217] Chang, *Can't Stop, Won't Stop*, pp41-59.
[218] Chang, *Can't Stop, Won't Stop*, pp58-65.
[219] Chang, *Can't Stop, Won't Stop*, pp67-85.

B-Girls, the graffiti artists, the rappers and DJs, eventually dubbed The Four Elements[220] – the opportunity to bring people together and stop the violence. He pivoted his gang, the Black Spades, into The Organization and then finally the Universal Zulu Nation, drawing on the teachings of the Nation of Islam, the Five Percenters and the Black Panthers to turn the block parties into an Afrocentric movement that preached a creed of 'Peace, Love, Unity and having fun'[221]. Once Charlie Ahearn's *Wild Style* (1982) film cemented the idea that the Four Elements were essential parts of one coherent whole, hip hop finally arrived[222].

In the 70s and 80s, Afrika Bambaataa was not only a global pop star but also the head of the first church of hip hop, and his ambitions weren't limited to the Bronx: he travelled the world to spread the Universal Zulu Nation's message[223], including to Covent Garden, London[224]. It was these visits across the 1980s that caught the attention of the UK media and meant that hip hop was notable enough to inspire the **Doctor Who** production team.

There is still some debate about whether UK hip hop was merely an imitator, or a parallel evolution born from similar social

---

[220] A fifth element of knowledge was added later.

[221] Chang, *Can't Stop, Won't Stop*, pp89-107. It has to be noted at this point that Bambaataa is no longer connected to the Universal Zulu Nation, after being expelled when a number of people made allegations of sexual abuse against him: see Beaumont-Thomas, Ben, 'Afrika Bambaataa Sued for Alleged Child Sexual Abuse', *The Guardian*, 10 September 2021.

[222] Chang, *Can't Stop, Won't Stop*, pp111-14, 141-65.

[223] Chang, *Can't Stop, Won't Stop*, p90.

[224] Procter, 'Old to The New Q&A'.

circumstances[225]; the SS Empire Windrush also brought dub and sound systems to the UK, and the UK government's attitude to its young, Black citizens was barely distinguishable from New York's, particularly if they lived in the North of England[226]. In the UK, the Caribbean was more of an influence than it was in the US[227], with patois and toasting common in early UK hip hop. But it would be churlish to suggest that US hip hop wasn't also an influence.

Early US hip hop connected with a seven-year-old Armenian boy displaced by the Iranian Revolution, who had eventually found himself at Christ College boarding school in 1970s Blackheath. He worked his way through the four elements, heading to Covent Garden (along with the rest of the UK scene: Bristol's The Wild Bunch, Manchester's Broken Glass and Wolverhampton's West Side Crew all regularly made the journey to London[228]) to get involved with hip hop culture under the name Electron. Although he used to dance, he knew he was not at the level he needed to be, so beat-boxing and tagging became his focus, while also writing lyrics and teaching himself to MC by learning from the records he heard. Here is where he was gifted the name Blade[229]. Through the 80s, Blade became an MC and performed gigs in notorious venues like the Albany in

---

[225] See Emery, *Wiggaz with Attitude* p8 vs Qureshi, Arusa, *Flip the Script: How Women Came to Rule Hip Hop*, p24.

[226] Parker, Simon, 'The Leaving of Liverpool: Managed Decline and the Enduring Legacy of Thatcherism's Urban Policy'.

[227] Qureshi, *Flip the Script,* p44.

[228] Procter, 'Old to The New Q&A'.

[229] The name was suggested to him by a friend who later died tagging the Underground, and he kept it as a tribute. (See Allcity TaxiTalk Show, 'MC Blade Talks about the Early Years, LL Cool J, Chuck D Public Enemy, Mc Mello & Loads More'.)

Deptford, gaining attention from record labels keen to get a piece of the increasingly lucrative hip hop market[230]:

> 'I remember a record label had offered me a deal [...] and then when I went and met them and they saw I wasn't black they kinda backtracked [...] they politely said "We don't know what to do with a non-black rapper. We don't know how to market you".'[231]

Because of its origins – in particular, links with the teachings of the Nation of Islam, whose leader the Honorable Elijah Muhammad preached that the white man was the devil[232] – and despite hip hop in the US and in the UK having diversity in its fans and artists, being born from the coming together of Black and Puerto Rican youths, hip hop was seen as a Black sub-culture[233]. White fans were accepted – so many white teens were being drawn to it that Ice-T later referred to it as a suburban home invasion targeting white children's minds[234] – but there was always an unease about white rappers, who were viewed by Black and white fans alike the way that the court system

---

[230] Allcity TaxiTalk Show, 'MC Blade Talks about the Early Years'.

[231] Blade, author's own interview.

[232] Chang, *Can't Stop, Won't Stop*, p100.

[233] Chang, *Can't Stop, Won't Stop*, pp103-105. The Beastie Boys and 3rd Bass were both groups of young white men; Cypress Hill was formed by Cuban brothers Sen Dog and Mellow Man Ace being joined by American-Italian DJ Muggs. Meanwhile in the UK, The Stereo MCs were formed by three white men from Nottingham; The Brotherhood's origins were as a collective of rappers, DJs and dancers who were white, Black, Muslim and Jewish; Gunshot included White Child Rix, whose ethnicity was deemed important enough to explain in his name.

[234] Ice-T, 'Home Invasion'.

looks at Black barristers: a surprising oddity who had to be exceptional to succeed and really might be more at home on the other side of the divide[235] This looks to have been carried over into *The Greatest Show*: the rapping Ringmaster was 'described as a "Black Joe Cool"' in the first breakdown[236], and is the only Black actor in the story:

> 'I can't remember whether it was me or Andrew [that suggested the Ringmaster rap]. In our slightly clumsy way, I think we were trying to ensure that there was a bit more ethnic diversity in the casting of **Dr Who**.'[237]

Whoever it was, once it came to casting there didn't seem to have been much consideration given to whether or not Ricco Ross could actually rap:

> 'Although Ricco was a very good actor, he wasn't very comfortable with some of the dance aspects of the part. It was written for someone who had that absolutely at their fingertips [...] Ricco had to work very hard to get the rap opening.'[238]

With no disrespect intended towards Ross, this is something of an understatement. Rapping is a performance skill as much as acting is, and needs time, practice and dedication to master; Blade started rapping to his schoolmates in the early 80s, spending his downtime building his cardiovascular fitness to improve his breath control. It

---

[235] Emery, *Wiggaz with Attitud* pp206-211.
[236] *Griffiths,* 'Honk, the Squonk and a Green Non-Entity'.
[237] Stephen Wyatt, author's own interview.
[238] Stephen Wyatt in Griffiths, 'Oh What a Circus Oh What a Show'.

wasn't until *The Greatest Show* was being planned that he released 'Lyrical Maniac' (1988), his first single. He spent the next years selling his records to strangers on streets all over London to begin with, then expanded to wherever he could get to including some parts of Europe, slowly building his skills and his fanbase. He even achieved chart success later in his career after partnering with producer/DJ Mark B for the album *The Unknown* (2000)[239]. As such, showing him Ross' rapping as the Ringmaster is a little akin to showing Michelangelo my child's first drawings. But that didn't stop me doing it:

> 'He would not have survived at the Albany. That was actually embarrassing to watch. And especially since I recognised him as somebody who had been in something much bigger[240] [...] you could sense "why am I here". But what's sad is there were plenty of rappers out there that probably would have done that if they'd been approached. And they could've added some kind of [...] you know, if I'd done it and I did my own lyrics and stuff, then I would've been comfortable doing that. So what I'm saying is with this guy is they've taken someone who doesn't live that life and they've stereotyped him into a role.'[241]

This isn't entirely unexpected. Serious attempts to represent the UK's growing hip hop culture weren't unknown, but *The Greatest Show* was never likely to be one of them. Nor was it intended to be – this

---

[239] Allcity TaxiTalk Show, 'MC Blade Talks....
[240] One of Ricco Ross' credits prior to *Greatest Show* was *Aliens* (1986).
[241] Blade, author's own interview.

was something else: the Ringmaster's defining characteristic was that he should be 'cool', and in 1988 rapping and blackness were two things that were cool. Cartmel wanted **Who** to be seen as new, different, **relevant**, building a stable of writers he'd made friends with at the BBC Writers' Workshop or met through **Doctor Who** and who would follow him on his eventual promotion to the more popular show **Casualty**[242]. Werewolves and rapping Ringmasters were minor ways of serving this goal; one of the most successful was the introduction of Ace.

Ace was – like only Dodo before her[243] – designed to be a real, modern teenager. Ian Brigg's brief character breakdown, written at Cartmel's request when it had been decided that she would become the Doctor's companion, makes several references to her connection to contemporary London teens: Briggs insisted 'the more current and realistic her speech, the better,' despite acknowledging that really she should be a year out of date because she'd left London in 1987; her parents 'are an ordinary middle-class couple'; the document gives, probably for the first time, the oft-repeated fact that the character is 'based on three girls I know'[244]. Ace was grounded as a real teenager with real relationships from a real place, in contrast to previous companion Mel who was an enthusiastic computer programmer who never mentioned computer programming, had a

---

[242] Cartmel, *Script Doctor*, pp22, 90-92, 108; Sandifer, Elizabeth, *TARDIS Eruditorum Volume 7: Sylvester McCoy*, pp288-89.

[243] Which is pleasingly symmetrical, given that both characters apparently had similar names (Dorothea and Dorothy) and chose a nickname to disguise this.

[244] Briggs, Ian, 'Notes on the character ACE'.

mental ability that either doesn't exist or is exceptionally rare in adults[245], and never had her hometown mentioned on screen.

Another aspect of this comes from the way Ace was styled. Ace's outfit may have raised some eyebrows, but it is surprisingly contemporary[246]; the cover of the 19 October 1988 issue of *Just Seventeen* magazine features the Wee Papa Girl Rappers, two sisters who had started off as backing singers for Feargal Sharkey, pointing at the camera and smiling[247]. And they are dressed in the same black leggings and satin-effect bomber jacket that Ace wears on screen. Instead of badges, they have chunky jewellery, but young hip hop fans sometimes replaced the jewellery rappers wore with cheaper and easier to obtain badges[248]. Ace regularly carried a baseball bat, a uniquely American piece of sporting equipment that has alternative uses highlighted in Grandmaster Flash and the Furious Five's 'The Message'[249].

And then there is the boom box.

---

[245] That is, a photographic memory. See Foer, Joshua, 'Kaavya Syndrome' for a discussion of why it's unlikely Mel had his ability.

[246] So contemporary that it feels very out of place when she happily dons the jacket again in *The Power of the Doctor* (2022) - which, if Ace was 16 in 1987, would make her 51 years of age. This makes her the **Doctor Who** equivalent of the singer Tim Burgess having the same haircut since 1988.

[247] *Just Seventeen*, October 19 1988.

[248] Blade, author's own interview. Hip hop has a philosophical relationship with gold jewellery because of its connections with Africa and Black exploitation, which is worth investigating but unfortunately not relevant to the matter at hand.

[249] 'Junkies in the alley with a baseball bat' are threatening the song's narrator, who should not be pushed because he is close to the edge.

The portable tape deck that Ace hefts on her shoulder in any number of television stories started life as the Philips Radiorecorder in 1969, its dual innovations being a tape deck that could be used to record from the radio and that it was portable. Later models also boasted impressive volume, particularly at lower frequencies – the boom in the boom box. As hip hop grew in popularity, so the boom box became the music system of choice: its portability and sound profile meant it could be used on the street to play anything that could be recorded to tape, rather than being limited to radio that didn't always support underground hip hop. The boom box's popularity with black and Hispanic youths is what led to its derogatory nickname – the ghetto blaster didn't blast white suburban America – and it could still attract racist comment in the UK[250].

Despite the **New Adventures** cementing the idea that Ace likes the Happy Mondays and the Stone Roses, her choice of fashion and portable electronics suggests she's a fan of hip hop[251]. But I think it's possible to go further than that. Early UK hip hop fans were fairly welcoming, and early gigs – and bands – could happily accommodate white fans[252]; to be honest, it was hard enough finding other people who supported the local flavour over America's more prominent

---

[250] Hodgson, Stewart. 'The Story of the Ghetto Blaster: An Icon in Audio History'; Emery, *Wiggaz with Attitude*, p30.

[251] Cornell, Paul, *Timewyrm: Revelation*, pp12, 156; Cornell, Paul, *Happy Endings*, pp36-37. The latter also states that a young Ace enjoyed 'World in Motion', the England Team's World Cup song, which is pleasingly close to saying she enjoyed the 'Anfield Rap', co-written by Derek B, who will become important shortly.

[252] Emery, *Wiggaz with Attitude,* p33.

exports without introducing a race bar[253]. But hip hop was still predominantly Black, and introduced its white fans to ideas of racism and prejudice that they might not have come across otherwise, particularly if they weren't from the inner-city areas where hip hop was actually being made, and instead lived in relatively better-off suburbs like Perivale. This could give white fans an awareness of their whiteness[254] – as a white fan of NWA, you knew that you should never say their unacronymised name nor sing along to the majority of their lyrics – which could lead to guilt or oversensitivity[255].

This picture of a white hip hop fan would fit with Ace being one of the more racially aware characters in **Doctor Who**[256], but her decision to essentially[257] cosplay the Wee Papas might make her feel a little racially uncomfortable. Perivale, though, is an area in the borough of Ealing that had a large Asian and British Asian population in 1991[258]. And young British Asians also found themselves drawn towards hip hop, without the same baggage. As Nish Kumar recalls:

'There's a **Goodness Gracious Me** sketch with these two

---

[253] Emery, *Wiggaz with Attitude,* p132.

[254] Andrew Emery talks about feeling more comfortable receiving a reply from Gee Street after sending them his demo, for example, because as the home of the Stereo MCs they 'evidently didn't care if you were white' (Emery, *Wiggaz with Attitude*, p125).

[255] Emery, *Wiggaz with Attitude,* p79.

[256] Her rejection of Mike's racism in *Remembrance of the Daleks*, her history with Manesha in *Ghost Light* and the **New Adventures**, or even her guilt at using racial slurs under the influence of Morgaine in *Battlefield*.

[257] The closest census date to Ace's departure in 1987.

[258] See '2001 Census Key Statistics for Ealing' for a comparison of 1991 and 2001 in this respect.

characters called the Bhangra Muffins, who are two young South Asian guys... and [...] their identity is a sort of cobbled together mixture of Indian slang and references to Jamaican culture. [...] I guess because [...] there was really no popular cultural conception of what a South Asian was supposed to be like, right? And so there's a generation one up from us maybe had to sort of invent an identity that was like half based on things they'd overheard their parents say and either Reggae music or rap music.'[259]

Elizabeth Sandifer makes the point that Ace is 'a children's television version of an urban teenager', whose claims to being real and modern are somewhat undermined by her introduction as a waitress in an alien Bejams who time-travelled through the medium of homemade nitro-glycerine[260]. If Ace is as close to a real, urban, contemporary teenager as **Doctor Who** felt able to go, I'd argue it's possible that her costume, slang and boom box were as close to a British Asian hip hop fan as the show could face too.

And yet, to quote Blade:

'The only thing that makes you think there's a possibility of that is the badges on the jacket and the stereo, the ghetto blaster. But rock people used to walk around with ghetto blasters. Does [Ace] look like a UK hip hop fan? Did I look like a rapper? Is that even important? I don't know what the rules are: all I know is just because someone dresses a way, it

---

[259] Nish Kumar in Ranganathan, Romesh, *Hip Hop Saved My Life*.
[260] Sandifer, *TARDIS Eruditorum Volume 7*, p74. Sandifer sees this as one of the strengths of the character, and I have to agree.

doesn't mean they are that way.'

This shows the limits of **Doctor Who**'s efforts to appear more relevant, more youthful, by borrowing some of the aesthetics of youth and relevance. If it's ultimately too much for me to argue that Ace is **Doctor Who**'s first hip hop-loving British Asian companion because, if you ignore the fact that she isn't, she looks like she could be, it's also too much for the show to think it can borrow some of hip hop's cool because it has a Black man awkwardly reciting doggerel over a beat for a few minutes of screen time. Because the audience know what they're watching:

> 'When we were turning on the TV in the early 80s and we saw things like *Beat Street* [1974] and all that, we felt like OK, this is us being represented now. When we saw the real documentaries like *Style Wars* [1983] and all that kind of stuff, to us it was like wah they've got this right. But when you see things like [*The Greatest Show*], it's not the right way to be represented. And what that does in the long run is it dilutes what we're doing. So what happens is people that don't really know about hip hop will look at that and think that's what hip hop is, if that's the first thing they've seen.'

Hip hop is more than just a drum beat and some rhymes. There is a well-known concept of freestyling – ad-libbing lyrics in the heat of the moment – that has led to a general idea that all rap is made that way. MCs like Blade, however, take time on their lyrics, writing them down, testing them out, honing them[261]. Many of the stylistic and

---

[261] Blade, author's own interview.

linguistic tricks of modern poetry are put to work in hip hop lyrics – take, for example, this brief section of Blade's 'Bedroom Demo':

> 'Heads, now you get a taste of the double
> No trouble, you're just another one on the rubble
> I take a pillow and attack you
> And if I miss I get your mother to smack you.'[262]

At the risk of dissecting the frog, this is a classic piece of hip hop braggadocio, a humorous image of a rapper so skilled that even your own mother would happily step in to assist in beating you down on their behalf. But notice the length of the lines: all of them have a slightly different number of syllables, but in delivery each takes the same number of beats. This produces a counter-rhythm, syncopation behind the regular beat of the song's drums and baseline that makes the structure that much more complex. Notice the triple rhyme of double/trouble/rubble, where the middle rhyme occurs at the start of the second line: this repeats the syncopation trick, with the ear hearing each rhyme and building another rhythm to complement the two we've already identified. Notice the way the attack/smack rhyme occurs just before the end of the lines, with the sharp, short words shifting the emphasis away from the last beat. This complexity of rhyme, rhythm and structure is called flow in hip hop, and the best MCs play with it and make it unique to them.

Now compare that with the opening four lines of the Ringmaster's rap:

> 'Now welcome folks, I'm sure you'd like to know,
> We're at the start of one big circus show.

---

[262] Blade, 'Bedroom Demo'.

There are acts that are cool and acts that amaze.

Some acts are scary and some acts will daze.'[263]

These lines are obviously drawn out to expand simplistic content ('Welcome to the circus: the show's starting and we've got a variety of acts') so that they fit the meter, rhyme scheme and rhythm: 'I'm sure you'd like to know' is the kind of line that appeals to inexperienced MCs because it can be used in any context and offers an easy rhyme. The rhythm itself is much more fixed – only the use of 'amaze' stops each line from having 10 syllables, or alters the flow of the delivery at all. Rhymes only occur at the end of lines, in neat couplets that reinforce rather than syncopate the measured rhythm. With the mix of 10-syllable lines and rhyming couplets, the Ringmaster's rap takes on the structure of iambic pentameter, and so it's understandable that Ross' delivery leans more towards Shakespearian declamation than rap. It's not entirely Ross' fault that his delivery seems stilted and one-note: the rhythm of the rhyme leads him to it.

Just as much care is taken over a rapper's music. It is well known that hip hop innovated the practice of sampling, taking a section of an existing song and lifting it out to form the basis of the new. This isn't something that hip hop invented completely out of thin air: it is possible to see forebears of sampling in jazz or Tchaikovsky's quoting of earlier songs[264]. Sampling is often seen as parasitic – taking the best bit of someone else's creativity and stealing it, such as 'Rapper's

---

[263] Part One.

[264] *Digging the Greats*, 'Breaking Down 'Dynamite!' by The Roots | J Dilla Production'; *Composer of the Month*, 'Tchaikovsky Symphony Number 4'.

Delight' taking Chic's 'Good Times' baseline and looping it[265] – but at its best, it is transformative and can be just as complicated as a rapper's lyrics. A Tribe Called Quest's 'Award Tour' (1993) takes a brief section of Weldon Irvine's 'We Gettin' Down' (1975) where the organist is transitioning between phrases and makes it the bedrock of the song[266] DJ Premier based Mos Def's 'Mathematics' (1999) on a section of The Fatback Band's 'Baby I'm-a Want You' (1972)[267], but cuts and loops it into a mix of seven other samples that creates a complex, mathematical tune that perfectly complements Mos Def's lyrics[268].

The backing track for the Ringmaster's rap, like its lyrics, is less technically complicated. It was created in advance by composer Mark Ayres and played through for Ross to react to, although the actual rap was reproduced in post-production.

The track featured an ersatz scratch made on a tape machine using snippets of Frankie Goes to Hollywood's 'Two Tribes', and the music was based on a current chart hit of the time, Derek B's 'Bad Young Brother'[269].

---

[265] Although in the case of 'Rapper's Delight' this is a misnomer: the sample is in fact an interpolation, a musician replaying a section of another song on their own instrument.
[266] Whosampled, 'A Tribe Called Quest Award Tour'.
[267] Tracklib, 'Sample Breakdown: Mos Def – Mathematics'.
[268] Digging the Greats, 'The Insane Musical Math of DJ Premier and Mos Def'.
[269] *The Complete History*, p73.

Derek B was born Derek Boland in Hammersmith in 1965, and was in 1988 Britain's most successful native rapper[270]. 'Bad Young Brother' was his fourth single, his second taken from his only album, *Bullet From A Gun* (1988), and his second UK Top 20 single that year. He was signed to Phonogram and set up his own production imprint, Tuff City Records, to release the record. It was re-released later that year when American rap mogul Russell Simmons signed Derek to Rush Artist Management, home to major US acts like Run DMC[271], Public Enemy and LL Cool J. For a moment, it looked like Derek B might be the first UK rapper to break America. But then the moment passed, and when he died of a heart attack at the age of 44 he was mostly considered a footnote in the history of UK hip hop[272], despite being one of the artists who did the most to bring it to the attention of those outside of the scene, including apparently Mark Ayres.

But part of the reason why Derek B's legacy does not reflect everything he achieved as an artist is that he wasn't recognised for it at the time either. Hip hop had arrived with the shock of the new, a fully fledged lifestyle with fashion, language, dance moves and philosophy all combined into one. That was what made it so enticing to a new generation looking for their own thing, but it also made it an easy target for mockery and moral panic. In 1988, hip hop was still a niche hobby, and its fans were often called on to protect it from ridicule[273]. Its striking style was easy to parody, and fans could turn

---

[270] You may wish to argue the case for Slick Rick, who was also born in London, but I discount him on the basis that he moved to the USA at an early age and gained prominence over there.

[271] Featuring Simmons' brother, Joseph, aka the Run of Run DMC.

[272] Marshall, 'Derek B Obituary', *The Guardian*, 17 November 2009.

[273] Emery, *Wiggaz with Attitude*, p83.

on anything that invited public scorn. Not all of the attention Derek B brought in 1988 was favourable: it isn't coincidence that Harry Enfield's 'Loadsamoney (Doin' Up The House)' (1988) includes the line 'Derek B? On your bike!'.

Derek B started out as a DJ at clubs and Kiss FM before moving into rapping[274]: because of this, he was his own producer and DJ as well as MC. Already known as Derek B when DJing, in a flourish of theatre he created an MC alter ego[275]: The lyrics of 'Bad Young Brother' make it clear Derek B is the DJ, whilst his single 'Good Groove' names the rapper as EZQ/Easy Q. I remember the friend who had introduced me to hip hop excitedly telling me in 1988 that Derek B and EZQ were the same person, laughing that Derek B had been performing a concert and made the mistake of stepping out from behind the decks to take a bow and getting booed as the crowd realised his deception. The only problem with the story is that it patently isn't true: Derek B wouldn't be able to perform as Derek B and EZQ at the same gig without the crowd noticing long before his bow, and he most likely performed to a pre-recorded backing track in any case. Plus, he made no effort to hide the fact that he was his own DJ: there are three separate characters on screen in the 'Bad Young Brother' video: Derek B, EZQ and an unnamed hype man shouting things like 'Thank God they're here!'. All of them are clearly Derek Boland in different

---

[274] Marshall, 'Derek B Obituary'.

[275] This isn't unheard of in early hip hop, which borrowed the showmanship of prog rock and funk: Overlord X's X Versus the World (1990) featured vocal contributions from Sidekick and Lord V; Sidekick was X pitch-shifted higher; Lord V lower. (*Breaktothebeat.com* 'Overlord X Interview').

outfits[276]. But the story fit with the image I had of Derek B at the time as someone who wasn't quite the real thing, and so it went unchallenged.

As a fan of UK hip hop, I knew instinctively that my role was to champion the real thing and ridicule anything that fell outside of those narrow boundaries. I had to protect hip hop from itself, publicly, even if to the untrained observer it might look as if I was criticising the very thing I claimed to love. Perhaps that sounds a little strange to you, or perhaps you're picturing a young Chris Chibnall again.

Part of the problem with Derek B was that he rapped in an American accent: as well as being seen as Black, hip hop was undoubtedly American. That perception can be seen in *The Greatest Show* again: the Ringmaster isn't just the only Black character, he's the only American one. So it might seem strange that a UK hip hop fandom obsessed with authenticity would take against the adoption of a more authentic US twang in the UK, but they did:

> 'I remember when there was this thing about you know say the rappers back in the days a lot of them used to rap in American accents. I feel like we were at a bit of a dilemma though cos back then if we rapped in our own accents everyone's like "you've taken an American thing and you're trying to turn it into British and it don't work." But then you know after a few years they were like slagging us off for emulating what they pushed us to emulate.'[277]

---

[276] Derek B, 'Bad Young Brother'.
[277] Blade, author's own interview.

It isn't unusual for the UK to look to America for support and respect: Overlord X left Mango Records after two successful albums to sign with Motown, only to have them decline to release his third and ending his career as a solo artist[278]. Even **Doctor Who** was guilty of it: when John Nathan-Turner realised how close to losing his job he was, one of his solutions was to cultivate the show's relationship with American fandom[279] – indeed, Sophie Aldred had just returned from her first US convention appearance when filming for *The Greatest Show* began [280] . What it seems that Nathan-Turner failed to appreciate was that the nature of the BBC's charter meant that it couldn't make shows primarily for an overseas audience and he was actually increasing the likelihood of cancellation by courting US fandom over the UK[281]. UK hip hop fans at least recognised that they were the primary market for UK hip hop, and this was where the wariness of ersatz US accents came from.

The problem is that it isn't clear Derek B (or more accurately, EZQ) rapped with an American accent. Certainly, he doesn't entirely rap with his speaking voice, using a more nasal, higher register than he speaks with in his interviews[282]. But he frequently name checks London in his records, and doesn't seem to be mimicking the intonation or pronunciation of the New York accent that would have

---

[278] *Breaktothebeat.com*, 'Overlord X Interview'

[279] Sandifer, *TARDIS Eruditorum Volume 6*, p304.

[280] *The Complete History*, p65.

[281] Sandifer, *TARDIS Eruditorum Volume 6*, p304.

[282] He wouldn't be the only rapper to deliberately craft a rapping voice, though: B-Real of Cypress Hill has one of the most distinctive voices in Hip Hop, and he similarly decided to pitch his voice higher and more nasal to stand out from his bandmate.

been the mark of 'authentic' hip hop at the time: if he is trying to fool anybody into thinking he is from the US, he isn't doing it very successfully. Blade – an MC who very much **does** rap and speak with the same accent – was a contemporary of Derek B's and isn't convinced either:

> 'For me personally [...] I couldn't hear it but a lot of people used to [...] I think it's more to do with the pronunciation of certain words rather than the accent itself. Because he was obviously educated to a high level. So the punctuation and the elocution in what he was doing was not like the average person who just wanted to rhyme and flow sick. He moved to Woodford, which is kinda like a posh area compared to all the people that were living where we were living.'[283]

This might be moving closer to where the problem is. In its early days, hop hop wasn't a Black sub-culture: it was an underclass sub-culture. When it arrived in the UK, it was in inner-city London, Manchester, Bristol, Nottingham, Glasgow[284]. Many of the pioneers of UK hip hop were poor kids growing up in Thatcher's Britain, used to being told that the arts weren't for them: suddenly they found an artform that that they could use to express **their** lives, not the lives of 'the arty-farty wealthy folk'[285]. There was an expectation that MCs would be part of the underclass, and would rap about their lives and struggles. In the same way that the pressure was there to rap with an authentic accent, there was a pressure to rap about an authentic life. The

---

[283] Blade, author's own interview.
[284] Gee unet, 'The early stages of Hip Hop in London'.
[285] Procter, 'Old to The New Q&A'.

boundaries of what hip hop fans would accept as authentic were fairly narrow, and Derek B crossed over them.

> 'Generally back then there was like this stigma like you know like ah, he sold out. If you were around back then, the word sell out used to be used quite often. I think a lot of people kinda considered Derek B as a sell-out.'[286]

At a surface level, the concept of selling out in hip hop is about compromising yourself in order to make money: selling your soul for a few extra pounds. When LL Cool J – a creator of serious records about his life as an MC both before and again after – released 'I Need Love' (1987), he was a sell-out. That the single got him chart success on both sides of the Atlantic and won the Soul Train Music Award for Best Rap Single[287] only confirmed the fact. There were always fans ready to spot commercialisation and cry 'sell-out' in hip hop's early days[288], but being a sell-out goes deeper than just a simple financial transaction, and indeed it doesn't have to involve money at all. Gunshot's 'No Sell Out' (1991) lists any number of crimes the sell-out might perform, from miming to backing tracks, or not having hard enough lyrics, or fraudulently claiming a history and lifestyle that isn't truly theirs. Like any small community, UK hip hop felt that its members owed a certain respect back, a duty to represent who they were and where they came from accurately. And that began to affect the choices that other artists made:

> 'I think people attach stigmas to themselves. You know,

---

[286] Blade, author's own interview.
[287] '1988 Soul Train Music Awards'.
[288] Emery, *Wiggaz with Attitude,* p111.

because they're around certain people and there's certain kind of banter that goes on behind closed doors and whatever, they don't realise they put these barriers up. I'm not saying everyone did that, but some people definitely did.'[289]

The idea that UK hip hop required a specific creative mindset to be authentic, that it needed to be protected from ridicule by a wider public who couldn't see its appeal, led to a feedback loop. Artists could feel that their lack of commercial success proved that they were making real hip hop, and would wear it like a stamp of approval. In *The Pioneers* (2000), Chester P (of Leeds-based group Taskforce) talked about his ambitions for his music:

> 'I want my hip hop to be street, underground so that it's gonna reach people like myself. I don't want it to be reaching all these booshie kind of people. I want it to be reaching proper ghetto youths. I mean I want it to be going round the estates and so on; have little ghetto youths singing my tunes. I don't want no fucking suit and tie man in his Porsche playing my shit.'[290]

Perhaps this sounds a little counterproductive to you, and maybe you're even having a little chuckle at those foolish fan gatekeepers who were happily damaging the success of the very thing they loved. But this is the very environment that Andrew Cartmel inherited when he started working at **Doctor Who**. Fandom had been slowly growing since Tom Baker's departure, and fans had the idea that they knew what was best for **Doctor Who**. With one eye on the reaction to

---

[289] Blade, author's own interview.
[290] Chester P in *The Pioneers: The British Hip Hop Documentary*.

screenings at US conventions, and a fan (in the shape of Ian Levine) at the very heart of the production team, the idea of what good **Doctor Who** was slowly transformed and John Nathan-Turner and Eric Saward had spent their time relying more and more on the fans to keep the show on the air. They became victims of the same feedback loop. Cartmel's approach was to ditch the fanservice and focus instead on what made the show **Doctor Who**:

> 'We had a conscious junking of the mythology. Let's forget about the Master; let's forget about the Time Lords; let's get back to the original idea, which was [that the Doctor was an explorer in] outer space … there was a clean sweep.'[291]

UK hip hop wasn't as lucky: there was no Cartmel figure with the power to save it from itself. Despite cautious interest by some major UK and US labels, UK hip hop developed a fan-pleasing, hardcore strand sometimes called 'Britcore' that was by its very definition not particularly radio friendly[292]. In the days before the internet, this severely reduced the options for attracting new fans, as mainstream radio was one of the few places where people not looking for hip hop might discover it: pirate radio stations, records and gigs all needed to be sought out, and so largely catered for people who already knew what they were looking for. By clinging to the idea that mainstream success could only be embraced if the mainstream changed to accommodate UK hip hop and never the other way around, UK artists made themselves look like a risky investment. When The Turtles sued De La Soul for their 12 second sample of 'You Showed Me' on *3 Feet*

---

[291] Stephen Wyatt, quoted in Howe, Stammers and Walker, *The Doctor Who Handbook* vol 2, loc 11897.
[292] *The Pioneers*.

High and Rising (1989), demanding $2.5m and getting a hefty out-of-court settlement[293], it had a devastating impact on the UK hip hop scene. With political attention focused on hip hop's lyrics in the wake of the Watts Riots, major labels were pulling away from hip hop in the USA and the UK[294], and without major label support, UK hip hop artists could neither afford the costs of sample clearance, nor of being sued for not obtaining it. Some adapted, but others saw it as the end of the road, and UK hip hop's slow progress stalled.

The first age of UK hip hop came and went, never really breaking out of the underground, never selling out but never really selling either. Although UK hip hop had made steps towards the mainstream[295], that didn't translate into commercial success and by the middle of the 1990s it looked like it might have reached its peak[296]. When UK hip hop did finally get bigger successes, both at home and abroad, it was after a rebrand and with a new generation of MCs. And after the concept of selling out had been confined to history.

So where does that leave us? In a book that's supposed to be about **Doctor Who**, I've spent my last chapter talking mostly about UK hip hop. A form of entertainment from my childhood that delighted me with its ability to take snippets of the familiar and rework them into something new and creative, that I still love today. A form of entertainment that damaged its own potential to be successful because it chose appeasing fan gatekeepers over mass appeal, and

---

[293] Runtagh, Jordan, 'Songs on Trial: 12 Landmark Music Copyright Cases'.
[294] Chang, *Can't Stop, Won't Stop*, pp381-405.
[295] UK Hip Hop: The Story. '1985-1990: False Dawn'.
[296] UK Hip Hop: The Story. '1990-1995: Underground Years'.

defended itself against mainstream mockery by retreating further into niche appeal rather than address any legitimate criticisms. One that couldn't help looking to America to save it, but by the end of the 90s looked to be truly dead. One that didn't realise it had future success coming, once it stopped putting too much stock on what the fans thought and started making something that didn't feel like a relic from another time.

And instead I've been talking about UK hip hop.

There is a delightful confluence in the point at which Andrew Cartmel put in place all the things that let **Doctor Who** face its own Ragnarok and survive reborn – a period that he felt first came together in the story that featured the ritual sacrifice of the stereotypical **Doctor Who** fan – being the point that the show performed its boldest act of sympathetic magic and evoked UK hip hop as its spirit animal. But the magic was too successful: as UK hip hop's golden age passed by without mainstream recognition, so did **Doctor Who**'s reinvention, and neither would be properly appreciated until a new generation were ready to accept them. Perhaps it's fitting then that I give the last word on this period of my life to Blade:

> 'It is what it is. It's been and gone – can't live in the past, you need to move forward.'[297]

---

[297] Blade, author's own interview.

BIBLIOGRAPHY

Documents

Briggs, Ian, 'Notes on the character ACE'. October 1987. Provided by Ian Briggs.

Books

Aaronovitch, Ben, *Remembrance of the Daleks*. **The Target Doctor Who Library** #148. London, Virgin Publishing, 1990. ISBN 9780426203377.

Butler, Bill, *The Definitive Tarot*. London, Random House, 1975. ISBN 9780091210113.

Carpenter, Greg, *The British Invasion: Alan Moore, Neil Gaiman, Grant Morrison, and the Invention of the Modern Comic Book Writer*. Sequart Research & Literacy Organization, 2016. ISBN 9781940589077.

Cartmel, Andrew, *Cat's Cradle: Warhead*. **Doctor Who: The New Adventures**. London, Virgin Publishing, 1992. ISBN 9780426203674.

Cartmel, Andrew, *Script Doctor: The Inside Story of Doctor Who 1986-89*. Surrey, Miwk Publishing, 2013. ISBN 9781908630681.

Chang, Jeff, *Can't Stop, Won't Stop: A History of the Hip-Hop Generation*. London, Ebury Press, 2007. ISBN 9780091912215.

Cooray Smith, James, *The Ultimate Foe*. **The Black Archive** #14. Edinburgh, Obverse Books, 2017. ISBN 9781909031616.

Cornell, Paul, *Timewyrm: Revelation*. **Doctor Who: The New Adventures**. London, Virgin Publishing, 1991. ISBN 9780426203605.

Cornell, Paul, *Love and War*. **Doctor Who: The New Adventures**. London, Virgin Publishing, 1992. ISBN 9780426203858.

Emery, Andrew, *Wiggaz with Attitude: My Life as a Failed White Rapper*. Fat Lace Publishing, 2017. ISBN 9781999760700.

Garrison, Tom, *Norse Mythology*. London, Tom Garrison, 2023. ISBN 9798215424049.

Lane, Andy. *All-Consuming Fire*. **Doctor Who: The New Adventures**. London, Virgin Publishing. 1994. ISBN 9780426204152.

Howe, David J, Mark Stammers and Steven J Walker, *The Handbook: The Unofficial and Unauthorised Guide to the Production of Doctor Who Volume 2*. Tolworth, Telos Publishing, 2016. ISBN 9781845839420.

Marson, Richard, *Totally Tasteless: the Life of John Nathan-Turner*. Surrey, Miwk Publishing, 2016. ISBN 9781908630407.

Molesworth, Richard, *The John Nathan-Turner Production Diary 1979-1990*. Tolworth, Telos Publishing, 2022. ISBN 9781845831998.

Parkin, Lance, *A History of the Universe: From Before The Dawn of Time and Beyond The End of Eternity*. London, Virgin Publishing Limited. 1996. ISBN 9780426204718.

Pinch, Geraldine, *Egyptian Mythology: A Guide to the Gods, Goddesses, and Traditions of Ancient Egypt*. Oxford, Oxford University Press, 2004. ISBN 9780195170245.

Platt, Marc, *Battlefield*. **The Target Doctor Who Library** #152. London, Virgin Publishing, 1991. ISBN 978042620350.

Platt, Marc, *Lungbarrow*. **Doctor Who: The New Adventures**. London, Virgin Publishing, 1997. ISBN 9780426205029.

Qureshi, Arusa, *Flip the Script: How Women Came to Rule Hip Hop*. 404 Ink, 2021. ISBN 9781912489305.

Radford, Benjamin, *Bad Clowns*. University of New Mexico Press, 2016. ISBN 9780826356666.

Reed, Gary, *Book of Tarot*. Trajectory Incorporated, 2015. ISBN 9781632945594.

Rieder, John, *Colonialism and the Emergence of Science Fiction*. Wesleyan University Press, 2008. ISBN 9780819568748.

Russell, Gary, *Divided Loyalties*. **Doctor Who: The Past Doctor Adventures**. London, BBC Books. 1999. ISBN 9780563555780.

Sandifer, Elizabeth, *TARDIS Eruditorum Volume 6: Peter Davison and Colin Baker*. Eruditorum Press, 2015. ISBN 9781517376369.

Sandifer, Elizabeth. *TARDIS Eruditorum Volume 7: Sylvester McCoy*. Eruditorum Press, 2020. ISBN 9798681437581.

Wood, Tat. *About Time: The Unauthorized Guide to **Doctor Who** – Volume 6 – Seasons 22 to 26, the TV Movie*. Des Moines, Mad Norwegian Press, 2007. ISBN 9780975944653.

Periodicals

Doctor Who Magazine (DWM). Marvel UK, Panini, BBC, 1979-.

> Griffiths, Peter, 'Oh What a Circus Oh What a Show'. DWM #263, cover date 8 April 1998.

> Griffiths, Peter, 'Honk, the Squonk and a Green Non-Entity'. DWM #263, cover date 8 April 1998.

Doctor Who: The Complete History. Volume 45 *Silver Nemesis, The Greatest Show in the Galaxy*, and *Battlefield*. Cover date February 2016.

The Guardian.

> Beaumont-Thomas, Ben, 'Afrika Bambaataa Sued for Alleged Child Sexual Abuse'. *The Guardian*, 10 September 2021.

> Leith, Sam, '*Watchmen* Author Alan Moore: "I'm Definitely Done With Comics"'. *The Guardian*, 7 October 2022.

> Marshall, Vie, 'Derek B Obituary'. *The Guardian*, 17 November 2009.

> Robb, John, 'I Bet You Looked Good on the Dancefloor'. *The Guardian*, 6 October 2006.

> Summerscale, Kate, 'Top 10 Phobias and What They Reveal About The Strangeness of Life'. *The Guardian,* 2 October 2022.

Just Seventeen. EMAP, 19 October 1988.

Cornell, Paul, 'The Ashes of Our Fathers'. *Cosmic Masque* XIV, The Doctor Who Appreciation Society, 1991.

Eno, Vincent and El Csawza, 'Vincent Eno and El Csawza Meet Comics Megastar Alan Moore'. *Strange Things Are Happening* vol 1, no 2, May/June 1988.

Fulchignoni, Enrico, 'Oriental Influences on the Commedia dell'Arte'. *Asian Theatre Journal* Vol 7, No 1, Spring 1990, pp29-41.

Jordan, Peter, 'In Search of Pantalone and the Origins of the Commedia dell'Arte'. *Revue Internationale de Philosophie* Vol. 64, No 252 (2) 2010, pp207-32.

McConnell Stott, Andrew, 'Clowns on the Verge of a Nervous Breakdown: Dickens, Coulrophobia, and the Memoirs of Joseph Grimaldi'. *Journal for Early Modern Cultural Studies* Vol 12, No 4, Fall 2012, pp3-25.

O'Brien, John, 'Harlequin Britain: Eighteenth-Century Pantomime and the Cultural Location of Entertainment(s)'. *Theatre Journal* Vol 50, No 4, December 1998, pp489-510.

Stevens, Alan, and Fiona Moore, '47 Cool Things About *The Greatest Show in the Galaxy*'. *Celestial Toyroom* 450, 21 October 2015.

Tso, Ann, 'English History as Jack the Ripper Tells It: Psychogeography in Alan Moore's *From Hell*'. *The Literary London Journal* Volume 15 Number 1, Spring 2018.

Television

Doctor Who. BBC, 1963-.

'Meanwhile in the TARDIS'. Series 5 DVD extra, 2014.

The Pioneers: The British Hip Hop Documentary. 40 Oz Productions, 2000.

Open Air. BBC TV.

Episode #1.29, 8 December 1986.

World in Action. Granada Television.

No Porsche for Derek B, 7 November 1988.

Music

Blade, 'Bedroom Demo'. *The Lion Goes from Strength to Strength*, 691 Influential. 1993.

Enfield, Harry, 'Loadsamoney (Doin' Up The House)'. 1988.

Ice-T. 'Home Invasion'. 1993.

Web

'1988 Soul Train Music Awards'. http://awardsandwinners.com/category/soul-train-music-awards/1988/. Accessed 29 May 2023.

'2001 Census Key Statistics for Ealing'. https://www.ealing.gov.uk/download/downloads/id/2741/borough _profile-census_2001. Accessed 29 May 2023.

A Brief History of Time (Travel).

> Sullivan, Shannon Patrick, *'The Curse of Fenric'. A Brief History of Time (Travel)*. http://www.shannonsullivan.com/drwho/serials/7m.html. Accessed 20 November 2022.

> Sullivan, Shannon Patrick. 'The Greatest Show in the Galaxy'. *A Brief History of Time (Travel)*. http://www.shannonsullivan.com/doctorwho/serials/7j.ht ml. Accessed 7 June 2023.

> Sullivan, Shannon, '**Doctor Who**: The Lost Stories (The Seventh Doctor)'. *A Brief History of Time (Travel)*. http://www.shannonsullivan.com/drwho/lost/lost7.html. Accessed 5 January 2023.

British Hip Hop.

'1985-1990: False Dawn'.
https://old.britishhiphop.co.uk/ukhiphop/story/false_dawn.
htm. Accessed 1 November 2022.

'1990-1995: Underground Years'.
https://old.britishhiphop.co.uk/ukhiphop/story/undergroun
d_years.htm. Accessed 1 November 2022.

'coulrophobia (n.)'. *Online Etymology Dictionary*, 4 October 2016.
https://www.etymonline.com/word/coulrophobia. Accessed 30
December 2022.

'Creepy Clown Craze: How Dangerous Are Clowns Really?' BBC
News, 12 October 2016. https://www.bbc.co.uk/news/world-us-
canada-37628664. Accessed 14 May 2023.

Doctor Who Location Guide.

'Season Twenty-Four'. 7 April 2013.
https://www.doctorwholocations.net/stories/24. Accessed
29 October 2022.

'Season Twenty-Five'. 7 April 2013.
https://www.doctorwholocations.net/stories/25. Accessed
29 October 2022.

'Season Twenty-Six'. 7 April 2013.
https://www.doctorwholocations.net/stories/26. Accessed
29 October 2022.

'The Enclosure Act. History of Western Civilisation II'.
https://courses.lumenlearning.com/suny-hccc-
worldhistory2/chapter/the-enclosure-act/. Accessed 14 May 2023.

'Fitzroy Speaks With Jessie Tsang'. *The Soul Survivors Magazine*. https://btpubs.co.uk/publication/?i=516603&article_id=3155628& view=articleBrowser. Accessed 1 November 2022.

'The Golden Oldie Picture Show'. *BBC Genome*. https://genome.ch.bbc.co.uk/5b197c6e49194bde9b1a469d220b41 57. Accessed 9 January 2023.

'Goldie'. *Back to the Old Skool*, 4 December 2008. https://www.backtotheoldskool.co.uk/index.php?option=com_cont ent&view=article&id=34:goldie&catid=7&Itemid=114. Accessed 31 October 2022.

'How Britain Voted Since October 1974'. Ipsos, 12 May 2010. https://www.ipsos.com/en-uk/how-britain-voted-october-1974. Accessed 8 December 2022.

'John Nathan-Turner.' *The Times*, 7 May 2002. https://cuttingsarchive.org/index.php/John_Nathan-Turner. Accessed 25 November 2022.

'Moon Hermit | 046'. *Mandatory Redistribution Party*, April 27 2020. https://mandatoryredistributionparty.podbean.com/e/moon-hermit-046/. Accessed 5 November 2022.

NASA.

>'Exoplanets'. 25 February 2023. https://exoplanets.nasa.gov/. Accessed 25 February 2023.

>'Planets'. 8 February 2023. https://solarsystem.nasa.gov/planets/overview/. Accessed 25 February 2023.

'What is an Exoplanet?' 13 April 2022.
https://exoplanets.nasa.gov/what-is-an-exoplanet/planet-types/overview/. Accessed 25 February 2023.

National Viewers' and Listeners' Association Archive. University of Essex, 25 July 2022. https://library.essex.ac.uk/NVALA. Accessed 13 May 2023.

'Overlord X Interview'. *Breaktothebeat.com*, 25 April 2012.
https://www.breaktothebeat.com/british-hip-hop-pioneers/overlord-x-interview/. Accessed 1 November 2022.

'Programme Index'. *BBC Genome*. 14 December 1988.
https://genome.ch.bbc.co.uk/330fb304a38243cb94d81a099e35ba1d.

'Recap / **Doctor Who** S25 E4 *The Greatest Show in the Galaxy*'. TV Tropes.
https://tvtropes.org/pmwiki/pmwiki.php/Recap/DoctorWhoS25E4TheGreatestShowintheGalaxy. Accessed 13 May 2023.

'Tchaikovsky Symphony Number 4'. *Composer of the Month*.
https://www.composerofthemonth.com/tchaikovsky-fourth-symphony. Accessed 5 November 2022.

Whosampled.

'A Tribe Called Quest Award Tour'.
https://www.whosampled.com/sample/2662/A-Tribe-Called-Quest-Trugoy-the-Dove-Award-Tour-Weldon-Irvine-We-Gettin%27-Down/. Accessed 18 October 2022.

'Derek B Bad Young Brother'.
https://www.whosampled.com/sample/331133/Derek-B-

Bad-Young-Brother-Beastie-Boys-Rhymin-%26-Stealin/.
Accessed 18 October 2022.

Youtube.

Allcity TaxiTalk Show, 'MC Blade Talks about the Early Years,
LL Cool J, Chuck D Public Enemy, Mc Mello & Loads More'. 27
June 2018.
https://www.youtube.com/watch?v=u_nPz5UKY3k&t=3928s
. Accessed 17 October 2022.

Derek B, 'Bad Young Brother'. 24 July 2012.
https://www.youtube.com/watch?v=6nGsiM-8hiE. Accessed
18 October 2022.

Digging the Greats, 'Breaking Down 'Dynamite!' by The
Roots | J Dilla Production'. 3 November 2022.
https://www.youtube.com/watch?v=zYQswIkRB7A.
Accessed 4 November 2022.

Digging the Greats, 'The INSANE Musical Math of DJ Premier
and Mos Def', 12 January 2023.
https://www.youtube.com/watch?v=Imm_zF8BG1s&t=915s.
Accessed 12 January 2023.

Gee unet, 'The early stages of Hip Hop in London: interview
with MC Mello'. 19 June 2012.
https://www.youtube.com/watch?v=h4VeKfQpmZ0.
Accessed 31 October 2022.

Sao Til, 'What was the Cartmel Masterplan? | **Doctor Who**'.
23 August 2020.
https://www.youtube.com/watch?v=HgIU6TgEEtg. Accessed
15 November 2022.

Grodvin, 'The Golden Oldie Picture Show, 1985, Part 2'. 4 February 2012. https://www.youtube.com/watch?v=__-cl_oM_lM&ab_channel=grodvin. Accessed 9 January 2023.

TheObsessedWhovian95, '**Doctor Who** Retrospective 10: The Cartmel Master Plan'. 13 June 2014. https://www.youtube.com/watch?v=DAOmfPTSVBo&t=132s. Accessed 15 November 2022.

Tracklib. 'Sample Breakdown: Mos Def – Mathematics'. 19 September 2021. https://www.youtube.com/watch?v=--A_89lTuiA. Accessed 18 October 2022.

Adam and Erik. *The Real McCoy Podcast.* 'The Greatest Show in the Galaxy', 16 March 2020. https://therealmccoy.libsyn.com/the-greatest-show-in-the-galaxy. Accessed 29 May 2023.

Babcock, Jay, 'Magic Is Afoot: A Conversation with Alan Moore About the Arts and the Occult'. *Arthur*, May 2003. https://arthurmag.com/2007/05/10/1815/. Accessed 14 November 2022.

Carter, Lynda, tweet sent 7:49pm, 27 September 2022. https://twitter.com/reallyndacarter/status/1574833527920762880. Accessed 25 October 2022.

Durn, Sarah, 'The Long, Hidden History of the Viking Obsession with Werewolves'. *Atlas Obscura*, 27 October 2021. https://www.atlasobscura.com/articles/hidden-history-viking-wolf-warrior-werewolf. Accessed 20 November 2022

Fava, Antonio. 'THE COMMEDIA MUST GO ON'. *Ars Comedica*. http://www.antoniofava.com/en/. Accessed 7 June 2023.

Foer, Joshua, 'Kaavya Syndrome'. *Slate*, 27 April 2006. https://slate.com/technology/2006/04/no-one-has-a-photographic-memory.html. Accessed 17 October 2022.

Hadoke, Toby, '**Doctor Who**: Too Much Information 1.1 – *An Unearthly Child*'. **Doctor Who: Toby Hadoke's Time Travels**, 25 December 2020. Accessed 10 December 2022.

Ho, Elizabeth, 'Postimperial Landscapes, "Psychogeography" and Englishness in Alan Moore's Graphic Novel *From Hell: A Melodrama in Sixteen Parts*'. Cultural Critique, 63. 2006. https://www.jstor.org/stable/4489248. Accessed 14 November 2022.

Hodgson, Stewart, 'The Story of the Ghetto Blaster: An Icon in Audio History'. *Audio Fidelity*. https://radiofidelity.com/the-story-of-the-ghetto-blaster/. Accessed 17th October 2022.

Hussey, Dr Kristin, '"Fools and Savages Explain: Wise Men Investigate" Sir William Withey Gull'. *Royal College of Physicians*. https://history.rcplondon.ac.uk/blog/fools-and-savages-explain-wise-men-investigate-sir-william-withey-gull. Accessed 12 February 2023.

Langley, Travis 'The Lost Origin of Coulrophobia, the Abnormal Fear of Clowns'. *Psychology Today*, 24 February 2017. https://www.psychologytoday.com/gb/blog/beyond-heroes-and-villains/201702/the-lost-origin-coulrophobia-the-abnormal-fear-clowns. Accessed 30 December 2022.

Lewis, Pete, 'MC Duke: The Originator'. *Blues and Soul* Issue 1101. http://www.bluesandsoul.com/feature/619/mc_duke_the_originator/. Accessed 1 November 2022.

Luiz, HC, 'Top Secret Clown Business: Six of the Scariest Clowns in Horror Movies'. *Bloody Disgusting*, 2 May 2022. https://bloody-disgusting.com/editorials/3713162/scariest-clowns-in-horror-movies/. Accessed 14 May 2023.

Margaritoff, Marco, 'Jack The Ripper's "From Hell" Letter and The Macabre Story Behind It'. *All That's Interesting*, 29 July 2021. https://allthatsinteresting.com/from-hell-letter. Accessed 14 May 2023.

Marshall, Rick. 'No Laughing Matter: The Scariest Clowns from Movies and TV'. *Digitaltrends*, 13 September 2019. https://www.digitaltrends.com/movies/scariest-killer-clowns-tv-movies/. Accessed 14 May 2023.

Martin, Tim, 'Everything and Moore'. *Aeon*, 17 October 2014. https://aeon.co/essays/alan-moore-i-am-in-charge-of-this-universe. Accessed 17 February 2023.

McCallum, Simon, 'Beyond the Tombstone: How British TV Responded to the AIDS crisis'. BFI, 12 February 2021. https://www.bfi.org.uk/features/british-tv-aids-crisis. Accessed 25 November 2022.

Ó Méalóid, Pádraig, 'Alan Moore's Secret Q&A Cult Exposed! Part IV: At Last the Truth Can Be Told!!!!!' *The Beat*, 16 October 2016. https://www.comicsbeat.com/alan-moores-secret-qa-cult-exposed-part-iv-at-last-the-truth-can-be-told/. Accessed 17 February 2023.

Orthia, Lindy, 'Enlightenment Was the Choice: **Doctor Who** and the Democratisation of Science'. *Research Gate*. https://www.researchgate.net/publication/300901891_Enlightenm

ent_was_the_choice_Doctor_Who_and_the_Democratisation_of_S
cience. Accessed May 2020.

Parker, Simon, 'The Leaving of Liverpool: Managed Decline and the
Enduring Legacy of Thatcherism's Urban Policy'. LSE, 17 January
2019. https://blogs.lse.ac.uk/politicsandpolicy/the-leaving-of-
liverpool/. Accessed 11 November 2022.

Platt, Marc. 'Introduction' to *Lungbarrow*. BBC Cult.
https://web.archive.org/web/20100131063430/http://www.bbc.co
.uk/doctorwho/classic/ebooks/lungbarrow/introduction/. Accessed
15 November 2022.

Procter, Ryan, 'Old To The New Q&A – MC Mell'O (Part One)'. *Old To
The New – Ryan Proctor's Beats, Rhymes & Hip-Hop Nostalgia*, 17
May 2011. https://oldtothenew.wordpress.com/2011/05/17/old-to-
the-new-qa-mc-mello-part-one/. Accessed 31 October 2022.

Procter, Ryan, 'Old To The New Q&A – MC Mell'O' (Part Two)'. *Old
To The New – Ryan Proctor's Beats, Rhymes & Hip-Hop Nostalgia*, 9
June 2011. https://oldtothenew.wordpress.com/2011/06/09/old-
to-the-new-qa-mc-mello-part-two/. Accessed 31st October 2022.

Ranganath, Romesh, 'Nish Kumar'. *Hip Hop Saved My Life* Season 4,
Episode 5. https://podcasts.apple.com/gb/podcast/s4-ep-5-nish-
kumar/id982388481?i=1000531785985, Accessed 29 October
2022.

Rooks, comment on *Digital Spy Forum*, 26 June 2007.
https://forums.digitalspy.com/discussion/comment/15701488#Co
mment_15701488. Accessed 25 November 2022.

Silman, Jon, 'How Did John Wayne Gacy Fit into the Origin of the
"Evil Clown"?' *Oxygen True Crime*, 29 October 2018.

https://www.oxygen.com/martinis-murder/how-did-john-wayne-gacy-fit-into-the-origin-of-the-evil-clown. Accessed 14 May 2023.

Ranger, 'We May Laugh Together Yet'. Tumblr, 29 January 2020. https://thirddoctor.tumblr.com/post/190530833430/doctor-who-killed-off-a-fictionalised-version-of. Accessed 4 December 2022.

Romano, Aja. 'The Great Clown Panic of 2016 is a Hoax. But the Terrifying Side of Clowns Is Real.' *Vox*, 12 October 2016. https://www.vox.com/culture/2016/10/12/13122196/clown-panic-hoax-history. Accessed 5 January 2023.

Rodriguez McRobbie, Linda, 'The History and Psychology of Clowns Being Scary'. *Smithsonian Magazine*, 31 July 2013. https://www.smithsonianmag.com/arts-culture/the-history-and-psychology-of-clowns-being-scary-20394516/. Accessed 14 May 2023.

Runtagh, Jordan, 'Songs on Trial: 12 Landmark Music Copyright Cases'. *Rolling Stone*, 8 June 2016. https://www.rollingstone.com/politics/politics-lists/songs-on-trial-12-landmark-music-copyright-cases-166396/the-beach-boys-vs-chuck-berry-1963-65098/. Accessed 1 November 2022.

Tocci, Jason, 'Geek Cultures: Media and Identity in the Digital Age'. University of Pennsylvania, 2009. https://repository.upenn.edu/cgi/viewcontent.cgi?article=2112&context=edissertations. Accessed 4 December 2022.

Tikkanen, Amy, '10 Famous Clowns: From Comical to Creepy'. *Britannica*. https://www.britannica.com/list/10-famous-clowns-from-comical-to-creepy. Accessed 14 May 2023.

TSV.

Bishop, David, 'Andrew Cartmel Interview'. *TSV* 40, 1 August 1994. https://doctorwho.org.nz/archive/tsv40/andrewcartmel.html. Accessed 14 November 2022.

Bishop, David. 'A Conversation with Paul Cornell'. *TSV* 28, April 1992. https://doctorwho.org.nz/archive/tsv28/paulcornell.html. Accessed 15 November 2022.

Vollmar, Rob, 'Northampton Calling: A Conversation with Alan Moore'. *World Literature Today*, January 2017. https://www.worldliteraturetoday.org/2017/january/northampton-calling-conversation-alan-moore-rob-vollmar. Accessed 9 October 2022.

Williams, Matt, 'There Could Be Four Hostile Civilizations in the Milky Way, Researcher Speculates', Phys.org, 16 June 2022. https://phys.org/news/2022-06-hostile-civilizations-milky-speculates.html. Accessed 16 February 2023.

Wolfe, Joanna M, Javier Luque and Heather D Bracken-Grissom, 'How to Become a Crab: Phenotypic Constraints on a Recurring Body Plan'. *BioEssays* Volume 43, Issue 5, May 2021. https://onlinelibrary.wiley.com/doi/abs/10.1002/bies.202100020. Accessed 16 February 2023.

Yung, E Alex, 'The 21-Year History of the Song "99 Problems"' *The Vulture*, 7 July 2014. https://www.vulture.com/2014/06/complete-history-99-problems-jay-z-ice-t.html. Accessed 2 November 2022.

ACKNOWLEDGEMENTS

This book would not have been possible without the willingness of Stephen Wyatt and Blade to give their time to help me out.

Able assistance was also provided by Ian Briggs, James Cooray-Smith, Stuart Douglas, Ian Potter, Philip Purser-Hallard, and Matt West.

And a tip of the hat to Jason Miller, who kept my brain ticking over throughout the writing process.

BIOGRAPHY

Dale Smith is a writer and web-developer, and so accordingly the best information about him can be found on his website at https://dalesmithonline.com.

He was born in Leicester, and now lives in Manchester. His previous **Black Archive**, *The Talons of Weng-Chiang*, featured fewer references to 1990s hip hop.